THE ACHARNIANS

The Complete Greek Comedy
Edited by William Arrowsmith

Aristophanes

The Acharnians

Translated by Douglass Parker
with sketches by Geraldine Sakall

Ann Arbor
The University of Michigan Press

Published in the United States of America by
The University of Michigan Press and simultaneously
in Toronto, Canada, by Ambassador Books Limited.

Library of Congress Catalog Card No. 61-12768

Manufactured in the United States of America
by The Haddon Craftsmen, Inc., Scranton, Pa.

Designed by George Lenox

SAGITTARIO

ΕΥΡΙΠΙΔΑΡΙΣΤΟΦΑΝΙΖΟΝΤΙ

VERBERATORI SUO

VAPULARIS INTERPRES

D. D. V. S. L. L. M.

CONTENTS

Introduction

The Play

The Acharnians was first produced at Athens early in 425 B.C.—the sixth year of the Peloponnesian War. About it we may make two initial statements:

    1) It is Aristophanes' earliest extant play.

    2) Its chief message is an argument for Peace.

These are undisputed facts, and it is perhaps curious that their fusion should create a hurdle to critical understanding of the play. But hurdle there is. By (1), literary history, which still probes with the clammy finger of nineteenth-century idealistic materialism, is compelled to find a certain primitiveness here, so that the poet's art will show an ascending organic development to the *Birds* and, later, the *Frogs*. In (2) the solution to this problem is found. Though the *Acharnians* is, it is suggested, too excellent in its parts for wholesale censure, it can still be relegated to the second rank on grounds of structure, by a strain of reasoning that runs somewhat as follows: "The play is about Peace. But the protagonist achieves Peace by the middle of the play—which therefore outruns its theme and is inferior to *The Frogs* or even the *Lysistrata,* which encompass their messages with nothing left over."

Curious reasoning, but not intrinsically impossible. Any cursory look at our play would appear to bear it out. Thus, the Chorus's address to the audience, the Parabasis, splits the play. In the first half, the old farmer Dikaiopolis ("Just-City") engages in a successful uphill fight to attain Peace; in the second, he proceeds to reap its fruits. The first half contains the argument, particularly the deservedly famous speech of Dikaiopolis to the audience, which justifies the Spartans; the second is made up of a series of farcical scenes, completely hedonistic in content with little or no political reference at all. A humpbacked product, many conclude; brilliant but artistically faulty pamphleteering, where the end does not follow from the beginning.

Logically, this is not indefensible. Empirically, it is an impossible judgment, violating any reasoned experience of the play, and utterly failing to explain certain foreign elements which swell even the first half of the play. Why, for instance, the visit to Euripides, the beggar's clothes, the relentless parody? What has this sort of aesthetic statement to do with War *or* Peace? And *is* the second part of the play merely farcical scenes in a random order?

Our answers begin to appear in the opening soliloquy, a hedonistic calculus which establishes the fundamental polarity of the play: Pleasure—Pain. The joys and sorrows totted up by Dikaiopolis in the first sixteen lines are purely aesthetic and can in no way be laid to the account of War or Peace. After this initial statement follow the pleasures and pains of the flesh, and for these Peace and War are responsible: the expansiveness of the country town against the stinginess of the enforced home, Athens proper. The presentation of the Peace as wine (via a latent pun in the Greek *spondai*—"libations" and hence "truce") welds cause and effect together, playing off the repeated complaint about war, which "cut down the vines." And the visit to Euripides, the acquiring of the rags—these ally the bad art bemoaned at the play's beginning, the flapping fustian, with the scrannel misery, war-born, at which our hero Dikaiopolis rebels. And, in Lamachos, the same rodomontade unites with jingoistic militarism, and hence with war itself.

In these terms the play is set, and in these terms it develops after the Parabasis. We do not here have unconnected scenes in no particular order, but a steady rise of Dikaiopolis on the scale of pleasure. Overt politics taken care of, we now see Dikaiopolis proceed from an initial success over the dirt-poor Megarian to a greater one over the prosperous Theban, after which he can demonstrate briefly his superiority to the average Athenian, rich or poor, rural or urban, and then plunge into the penultimate scene with Lamachos—the armoring scene—where Peace, plenty, and comedy lock in deadly stichomythia with War, poverty, and tragic gush. And, in the last scene, tragic hero, reduced to ridiculous wretchedness by war, confronts comic hero, exalted by drinking the very wine which is Peace, and the victory of Dikaiopolis is complete. Peace has defeated War, pleasure has put down pain, good art has overcome bad.

The reason for the thoroughgoing parody of Euripides' *Telephos*, a play produced in 438, thirteen years before the *Acharnians*, at length becomes plain. The King of Mysia who led the Greeks to war is metamorphosed into the beggar who, by example, points the way to peace, and our comedy is a tragic reversal—or, rather, a reversal of tragedy. Not a lofty character brought low, but a lowly, miserable old man raised to the peak of pleasure and success. Throughout it all, the Chorus of Acharnians remains static in fortune (though changing in attitude)—a yardstick against which to measure the progress of Dikaiopolis. At their first entrance, they are old as he is old, wretched as he is wretched. Through the latter half of the play, they lust continually for the food, wine, and sex which he achieves—and, such is the fate of controls, they receive none. But Dikaiopolis, once aged, is now rejuvenated; younger, if performance means anything, than the prematurely decrepit Lamachos.

Certainly the *Acharnians* is about Peace, and *for* Peace. And we may forever wonder at the make-up of a citizenry that would not only allow the performance of such a play, in the depths of a life-and-death war, at a public festival (the Lenaia), but would also award it first prize in the comic competition. But we must not let this lead us into the critical syndrome which equates "message" with "plot" automatically. The *Acharnians* is a unity—a highly skillful unity—of intrinsically disparate themes around a central focus, the Pleasure-Pain antinomy. And Peace, while the most important part of this unity, is still a part. Aristophanes was a playwright first, and this is a play.

Translation

The language of this translation is American English; its aim is comprehensibility as poetry, drama, and humor to a putative educated Greekless *hearer*—though that such will exist is, admittedly, a fairly feckless hope. To this end, I have expanded where necessary and important, particularly in the core of the play, the *agōn*—Dikaiopolis' defense to the audience and his subsequent confrontation by Lamachos—where it seems vital to me that every shift of thought be understood. That this swells an already long speech to prodigious size, I do not deny; I can only plead that poetry, drama, and humor, individually and collectively, have no greater enemy than the footnote. Thus, areas of metaphor have been changed on occasion, or expanded, or supplemented, or sometimes suppressed entirely. The fact of a joke in the original has been considered as of more importance in translation than the particulars of that joke. Names which involve puns (as they do a good half of the time in Aristophanes) have sometimes been translated, as those of the individual Acharnians; sometimes left unchanged, as Dikaiopolis; sometimes changed completely, as in the case of the Persian envoy, whose name in Greek, *Pseudartabas*—"False (Persian) Measure"—appears here as *Shambyses* to convey the falseness and Persianness.

One difficulty in this particular comedy deserves mention. The action of the *Acharnians* is articulated throughout by a clash between Euripidean *Schwärmerei* and what, for the purposes of the play, we are to regard as normal speech. In default of any contemporary tragic diction that can be parodied—except by making it flatter, which is antithetical to Aristophanes' practice—I have had recourse to the same ranting fustian which, in one guise or another, has marked highfalutin windiness in English for at least 350 years. Further, since even the "normal speech" is declamatory rhetoric of a texture surpassed in English only by Ben Jonson, I have not attempted to render any part of the play into the flattest possible English, which has become the fashion. But English rhetoric needs more space to work in than Greek, and the result has inevitably been more expansion. I have often, therefore, lost the conciseness of this most concise play of Aristophanes. Unhappily—but I would rather be understood.

Finally, I have had in mind, throughout this translation, not the ancient Theater of Dionysos in Athens, but the normal present-day proscenium stage. This is not to say that I regard it as an improvement, but as a fact—a fact whose attempted reform in a translation of a difficult Greek comedy can only obscure more important things.

In short, in changing a myriad of details to gain the impression of the whole without recourse to footnote upon footnote, I have been falsely true. Which is not the same thing, I trust, as being truly false.

Text

The text is basically that of Victor Coulon in the Budé series (first published 1923), supplemented by those of Van Leeuwen (1901), Rogers (1910), Elliott (1914), and Cantarella (1953). "Supplemented" is no word to use for that fantastically enjoyable amalgam of useful knowledge and wild rhetoric, the edition (with copious notes and translation into glossematic Shakespearian) of W. J. M. Starkie (1909). Some important deviations are commented on in the notes. The division of speeches between the two Koryphaioi is due, in the main, to the work of John Williams White, whose long-ago study "An Unrecognized Actor in Greek Comedy" (*Harvard Studies in Classical Philology* 17 (1906), pp. 159 ff.) was utilized fully only by Starkie. More modern editors seem, at times, to live in fear of helping the reader.

Acknowledgments

I should like to express my gratitude to the University of California for the faculty grants which made possible the typing of several stages of the versions of both the *Acharnians* and the *Wasps,* and to a number of my colleagues, primarily Donald Johns, William Sharp, and Marshall Van Deusen, for supplying my rantings with a receptive audience and acute criticism. I am also indebted to two of my former students, Joseph Winkler and Theodore Gulesarian, for forever asking "Why?" and to Donna Lippert for complete complaisance and competence in the face of rather curious demands placed on a typist. The sum of my wife's contributions is too staggering to be enumerated (as any woman whose husband has tried to become an Athenian comic poet will know), and my gratitude is in proportion. The onlie begetter of this work, who added to the normal editorial functions that of licking his contributor into shape as a mother bear does her cub, is remembered in the dedication.

DOUGLASS PARKER

Characters of the Play

DIKAIOPOLIS, *an elderly Athenian*

A HERALD

OLYMPOS, *a peripatetic divine*

AN AMBASSADOR

SHAMBYSES

THEOROS

FIRST KORYPHAIOS

SECOND KORYPHAIOS

CHORUS *of aged charcoal-burners from Acharnai*

DAUGHTER *of Dikaiopolis*

WIFE *of Dikaiopolis*

KEPHISOPHON, *servant and secretary to Euripides*

EURIPIDES, *a tragedian*

LAMACHOS, *a military man*

A MEGARIAN

TWO LITTLE GIRLS, *daughters of the Megarian*

AN INFORMER

A THEBAN

NIKARCHOS, *an informer*

LAMACHOS' SERVANT

A FARMER

A BEST MAN

A MAID OF HONOR

A MESSENGER

MEMBERS OF THE ASSEMBLY	ODOMANTIANS	AMBASSADORS
EUNUCHS	SLAVES	WHORES

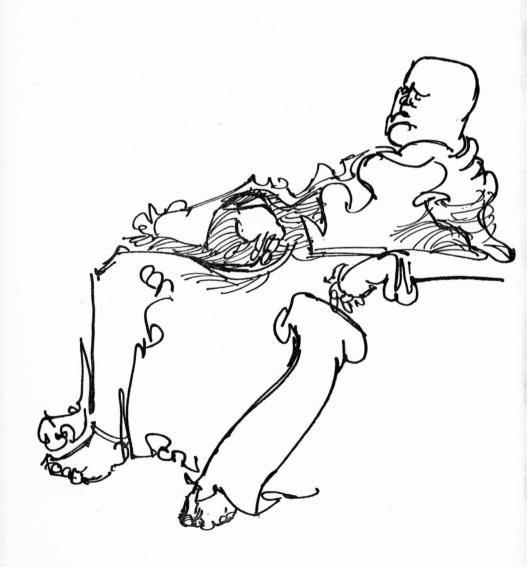

SCENE: *A street in Athens, representing, in the Prologue, the Pnyx—the meeting place of the Athenian Assembly. In the background are three houses, which belong, from left to right, to Dikaiopolis, Euripides, and Lamachos. Dikaiopolis, a disconsolate, ragged old farmer who has been forced into Athens to do sentry duty, is discovered alone before the Pnyx.*

DIKAIOPOLIS

Soliloquizing.

I have measured out my life in peptic ulcers.
Pleasures, sparse.
Quite sparse.

Counting on his fingers.

Precisely four.
But Sufferings—numberless:
my life is Destiny's Dump.
Come right down to it, what Pleasure have I known that truly
deserved the title of Unalloyed Joy?
The first
was that warm, satisfied, happy glow in my stomach
when I saw Kleon fairly caught in that comedy
by Aristophanes, compelled to belch up those five talents.*
That was a tonic. The Knights won my inexpressible
love for managing that. What a delicious day
for Hellas!
But that blessing was blotted out, of course,
by the torment of a terrible tragedy. Tingling in anticipation
of an Aischylos revival, aching and gaping in the audience,
I heard the announcement: *"THEOGNIS* WILL PRESENT HIS
PLAY."
Theognis? It felt more like Thrombosis, I tell you.
But I did have another Pleasure—Pleasure Two:
In the musical competition, I smiled to hear Dexitheos
sweetly drown out those jangling modern discords
with an old-time tune.
Not that *that* lasted, either.
(Doesn't anyone play *music* any more? This year
it was that foul-lipped flutist Chairis, sneaking in
with all those new-fangled trills. He murdered the hymn
and me. Death and a dislocated neck—
I ducked.)

Giving way completely to irritation.

But never, ever, since I began to wash,
have I been so bitten in my brows by soap as now,
when there's a stated meeting of the Assembly called
for dawn, and here's the Pnyx—completely empty!

Everybody's down at the Agora, gabbing, cackling,
running away from the Masters-at-Arms. Nobody's
going to rope *them* into their civic duty. No, sir!
The Executive Board* hasn't come!
                              Oh, it will—
late, shoving and jostling—you know how—
streaming down in a bunch to get the first bench;
but they don't give a damn for peace and how to get it.
Oh, Athens, Athens!
So I come to Assembly—as usual, first—and *sit*.
But what's to do when you're all alone?
                              Well,

Thinking and ticking his activities off on his fingers.
        I sigh,
            I yawn,
                I stretch . . .
                        sometimes I fart.
        I try to think of things to do . . .
                        I write . . .
        I pluck out my gray hairs . . .
                    I balance my books . . .

Becoming conscious of his finger-counting and thus his unhappiness,
he lapses briefly into declamation:
        I fix my eyes upon my fields and lust for Peace.
        I loathe the stingy, greedy city. I long
        for my own ungrudging countryside, my generous village,
        my openhearted home sweet home. *It* never barked,
        "Buy coal! Buy oil! Buy vinegar!" Gratis it gave me
        everything, unstintingly supplied my wants, and that blasted
        city byword "BUY"—
                    Goodbye to that!
        So here I am. By god, I'm ready to boo,
        to interrupt, to heckle every speaker who dares
        to say a word on any subject but Peace.

Commotion off-stage.
        Well, look! Here's the Executive Board—and it's noon.
        Didn't I tell you? Just what I was saying:
        Every last one of them pushing to sit up front.

Enter the citizens pell-mell, directed by a rather stuffy,
stentorian Herald. Olympos, a tattered, ascetic-looking*
creature, approaches cautiously.

        HERALD
        MOVE UP TOWARD THE FRONT! MOVE UP INSIDE
            PURIFIED GROUND!

OLYMPOS

Did anyone speak yet?

HERALD

Who wishes to address us?

OLYMPOS

Me.

HERALD

Who are you?

OLYMPOS

Me? Olympos.

HERALD

You're a god?

OLYMPOS

That's it,
an Olympian god. You see, Triptolemos and Demeter
conceived Olympos the first; he begat Keleos
who conceived a child by my grandmother Phainarete
and begat Lykinos, my father, and he begat me.*
Q.E.D., I am immortal, and the logical choice
to conclude a Peace with Sparta—in fact, expressly
commissioned by Heaven. But the Executive Board
refuses to pay my expenses. Can you imagine?
The gall of them—keeping a *god* on short rations.

HERALD

POLICE!

OLYMPOS

As two Skythian bowmen drag him off, kicking and screaming.

But I'm a *god,* I tell you, a *god!*
My great-great-grandfather was a god, my great-great-grandmother
was a goddess, my mother and father, even my uncles . . .

DIKAIOPOLIS

To the Executive Board.

Gentlemen, this is treason against the Assembly!
You can't arrest a man for opposing War
and promoting Peace!

HERALD

You, there! Sit down! Quiet!

DIKAIOPOLIS

Apollo, no, unless you listen to me now
and bring in a bill for Peace! Open debate!

HERALD

Disregarding him and looking off-stage.

THE AMBASSADORS FROM THE GREAT KING OF PERSIA!*

DIKAIOPOLIS

The Great King, yet!

                    I'm sick of all these embassies,
and Persian popinjays, and Asiatic hocus-pocus—

HERALD

SILENCE!

*Enter the Athenian ambassadors returned from Persia, dressed in
garish, outlandish misrepresentations of Persian* haute couture.

DIKAIOPOLIS

Oh, no! Holy Ekbatana, what a get-up!

The first ambassador advances and addresses the assembly.

AMBASSADOR

You dispatched us to visit the Great King's court
at a *per diem* salary of two drachmas a man—precisely
eleven years ago today.

DIKAIOPOLIS

                  Now I *am* sick—
eleven years of drachmas down the drain!

AMBASSADOR

Choked with emotion.

Let me tell you, it was a hard and bitter life
we led those long eleven years!
                     Ah,
that soul-sapping saunter across the plateaus, that endless
shade, deliciously beating down from the awnings,
that enforced recumbency in luxurious litters! We
were unmanned!

DIKAIOPOLIS

               Everything here was manned, of course—
by *me.*
          Ah, that ankle-snapping sentry-saunter
along the endless, littered City Walls!

AMBASSADOR

Nearly in tears.

And those pitiless Persian hosts! They compelled us to drink
sweet wine, wine without water, from gold and crystal
goblets—they actually made us drink it *neat!*

DIKAIOPOLIS

Oh, you poor addled Athenians! Don't you see
they're diddling you?

AMBASSADOR

Apologetically.

These Persian fellows, now—
they're not civilized, you know. True men, to them,
are those who excel in the pleasures of the festive board.

DIKAIOPOLIS

A status we reserve for adepts in buggery.

AMBASSADOR

After three years, we came to the Great King's court.
But there'd been a purge, and he'd evacuated,
for eight months' privy business in the Crapathians.*
He took his whole army to shit—Expense meant nothing.

DIKAIOPOLIS

I know, he's got piles. Anyone else would be wiped out
inside of a month. At most.

AMBASSADOR

—But when he returned,
He played the host as only the Great King can.
Ah, Magnificence! He served us up whole oxen
fricasseed in pots!

DIKAIOPOLIS

And heifer pie, I suppose.
—Fake! Humbug!

AMBASSADOR

—He set one bird before us
three times the size of Kleonymos. It was a *roc*,
they said.

DIKAIOPOLIS

Roc? *Rook* would be more like it.
You and your two drachmas a day!

AMBASSADOR

—And now,
we have returned to Athens with Shambyses,
councillor and confidante of the King himself,
one of those upon whose selves and services
the Grand Monarch so vitally depends, that they
are called the Very Eyes of the Great King himself.
I present, gentlemen, Shambyses, the Great King's Eye.

DIKAIOPOLIS
I devoutly wish that a raven would peck yours out—
the Ambassador's Eye.

HERALD

SHAMBYSES, THE GREAT KING'S EYE!

*Enter the Eye of the King, Shambyses. He wears Persian clothes
and a mask which depicts an enormous eye above and a beard below.
In spite of this—or perhaps because of it—he seems to have
some difficulty in seeing: he keeps moving his head from
side to side, walks slowly and unsteadily, and is escorted and
supported by two attendants dressed as eunuchs.*

DIKAIOPOLIS
Holy Herakles!

*Making a comparison between Shambyses' eye and the eyes normally
painted on the sides of Greek ships.*

By god, fellow, you certainly look shipshape.

*Shambyses, missing the lead of his eunuchs, gets tangled in his
cloak and falls.*

Doubling the cape, eh?

*The eunuchs carefully point the bogus Persian toward the
Executive Board.*

Well, safe harbor at last!

*Shambyses, dubious, stumbles, and is only saved by clutching
the Ambassador.*

That's it, tie up to the dock.

Dikaiopolis looks closely at the beard below the eye and flips it.

Your porthole's open.

AMBASSADOR
Very well, Shambyses. Inform us what the King
commissioned you to tell the Athenians. Proceed.

SHAMBYSES
Loudly and majestically.

ARTASHMEDLAP XARXES TWOGGLE SATRAP!

Dead silence.

AMBASSADOR
Somewhat nervously, to Dikaiopolis.

Do you understand what he's saying?

DIKAIOPOLIS

I'm no soothsayer.

AMBASSADOR

Relieved.

> Well. He says the King will send us gold.
> —Come on, now, speak up clearly about the *gold.*

SHAMBYSES

> WOAN GETTUM NO GOLDUM, GAPASSITY IONISH!

DIKAIOPOLIS

> That was certainly clear! We've been had again.

AMBASSADOR

> Well, what's he saying?

DIKAIOPOLIS

> What's he saying? He calls
> the Ionians gap-assed idiots if they expect
> to get any gold from Persia.

AMBASSADOR

Desperately.

> No! He's talking
> about the CAPACITY of all those bullion boxes!

DIKAIOPOLIS

> Bullion, balls!
> You cheap imposter! It's over!
> Get out of here! I'll grill this fellow myself.

*The Ambassador retires in evident confusion. Dikaiopolis plants
himself squarely in front of Shambyses and waggles his fist in
the face of the King's Eye.*

> Now look, you. A clear answer, with this in your face,
> or the Great King of Persia will have a bloodshot Eye:
> *Does* the Great King intend to send us gold?

Shambyses shakes his head. The two eunuchs jerk their heads back.

> We're being bamboozled by our ambassadors, then?

*Shambyses gives a single nod. The two eunuchs waggle their heads
up and down.*

> Look! These eunuchs nodded their heads in the Greek way.
> These aren't Persians—This is local talent.

Peering closely at the first eunuch.

> Eunuchs, eh? Better say *uniques.* I know *him.*
> It's limp-wrist Kleisthenes, the All-Athenian Boy!*

To the first eunuch, disgustedly.

> Do you even invert disguises! You took the advice
> of your rash and ready rump and shaved the wrong end!
> Eunuchs and beards are a contradiction in terms! Understand?

To the second eunuch.
> And who's this? Straton, maybe?

Complete confusion.

HERALD
> Silence! Sit down!
> THE COUNCIL SUMMONS THE GREAT KING'S EYE TO DINE
> IN THE EXECUTIVE HALL.

*The procession—ambassadors, Shambyses, eunuchs—collects
itself and exits.*

DIKAIOPOLIS
To the audience.
> By god, all this is enough
> to make a man choke! And then they squeeze me out here
> to cool my heels, to boot. But I've never seen
> the door that managed to shut *them* out from a dinner!
> Enough of this—the time has come for action,
> grand and awful.
> Where's Olympos?

OLYMPOS
Skulking back, considerably the worse for wear.
> Present!

DIKAIOPOLIS
> Here are eight drachmas. Take them and make a truce
> with the Spartans in *my* name. A private treaty,
> for me and my wife and children.

To the Assembly.
> As for you,
> send out all the embassies you want!
> Stand there forever with your mouths hanging open!

Exit Olympos on the dead run.

HERALD
> THEOROS, OUR AMBASSADOR TO THE COURT OF SITALKES!*

THEOROS
Effeminate and mincing.
> Here I *am!*

DIKAIOPOLIS
> The carpet's out for another swindler.

THEOROS
> We wouldn't have stayed in Thrace for *such* a time . . .

DIKAIOPOLIS
> I know: if you hadn't been drawing *such* a wage.

THEOROS
—if it hadn't snowed all over Thrace and simply made
the rivers *freeze*—

DIKAIOPOLIS
          —just about the time
Theognis was cooling off his audience here
with one of those frigid tragedies of his.

THEOROS
I passed the days in drinking with Sitalkes;
and you know, my dear, he's Philathenian to a *fault*—
simply *mad* about us all, so much enamored
that he scrawls on his walls, "The Athenians are *lovely!*"
His son—we made him a citizen—was, oooh, *wild*
to skin our Athenian sausages. He got down on his *knees*
and actually *begged* his father to send his adopted
country some aid and succor! Sitalkes swore
to help, to send us *such* an army we'd shout,
"Oooh, what a swarm of *locusts* is coming this way!"

DIKAIOPOLIS
I'm damned if I believe a single thing
you've said—except that bit about the locusts.

THEOROS
And now he's sent us the most *warlike* race in Thrace!

DIKAIOPOLIS
Oh-oh! I begin to see the light.

HERALD
               YOU THRACIANS,
WHO CAME WITH THEOROS, FRONT AND CENTER!

*Enter a detachment of Odomantians, notable for a hugeness of body,
a savage vacuity of expression, and an alarming length of violently
red-tipped phallus.*

DIKAIOPOLIS
                                      What's *this?*

THEOROS
THE ARMY OF THE ODOMANTIANS!

DIKAIOPOLIS
                          Odomantians?

Examining the troops more closely.
                             What happened here?

Who docked the Odomantian cock?

THEOROS

You pay these men
two drachmas each per day, and they'll ram and jam
Boiotia right into the *ground!*

DIKAIOPOLIS

Two drachmas a day?
For these walking appetites? They don't even come with foreskins!
And for *this* you'd turn your backs on our own Navy?

*During this exchange, some of the Odomantians have managed to
pilfer Dikaiopolis' garlic—the sole remains of his solitary
breakfast—divide it with their fellows, and begin eating it,
noisily. Dikaiopolis suddenly realizes his loss.*

Help! I'm ruined! I'm plundered! An Odomantian raid!
Drop that garlic!

THEOROS

Naughty! I wouldn't go near:
they're garlic-primed, like gamecocks—and, oooh, are they *game!*

DIKAIOPOLIS

To the Executive Board.

Gentlemen, are you going to stay in your seats
and do nothing, while I'm being robbed and maltreated
by a bunch of barbarians, here in the very heart
of Athens? I'm a citizen, remember?

Well?

*If the members of the Executive Board do remember, they give no
indication of it: there is no reply. First abashed, then annoyed,
Dikaiopolis tries a different tack. He sticks out his palm,
looks at it, looks at the sky, and announces:*

I move the Assembly adjourn, and table discussion
of the Thracians' wages.

It's a nondebatable motion—
Divine Intervention. Briefly, I've just received
a sign from Heaven—I felt a drop of rain.

This seems agreeable all around.

HERALD

LET THE THRACIANS RETIRE, TO RETURN DAY AFTER
TOMORROW. THE ASSEMBLY IS HEREBY DECLARED
ADJOURNED.

*General exit, in haste, by the Herald, the Executive Board, the
members of the Assembly, Theoros, and the Odomantians—in short,
by everybody but Dikaiopolis, who stands in center stage, looking
disconsolately about him.*

DIKAIOPOLIS

That's legislation for you:

I lost my lunch.

Looking off.

Look, here's Olympos back from Sparta already.
Welcome, Olympos!

OLYMPOS

*Entering on the dead run again, bearing three leather bottles.
Throughout this scene, he is very nervous, continually looking
back over his shoulder.*

No "welcomes" until I can stop.
Mind if I run? I have to keep fleeing to flee
those Acharnians.

Every bit helps, you know.

DIKAIOPOLIS

What's up?

OLYMPOS

Well, I was en route with the treaties, and someone
smelled them out—

true Acharnian elders, they were:
the real thing, hearts of oak, ribs of rock,
the authentic, genuine old maple-hearts
of Marathon. They set up a shout:

"You cesspool!
You dare bring a truce when our vines have been cut down?"
Then they gathered up rocks in their cloaks. I tried
to get away, but they kept following me
and shouting.

DIKAIOPOLIS

Let them shout. Have you got the treaty?

OLYMPOS

Producing his wine bottles.

But certainly. I have three samples right here.

Proffering the smallest bottle.

Here's the five-year vintage Peace. Taste it.

DIKAIOPOLIS

Uncorking and sniffing.

Pew!

OLYMPOS

What's wrong?

DIKAIOPOLIS

                There's caulk in it. It smells
of pitch and shipyards.

OLYMPOS

Proffering a somewhat larger bottle.

                All right, here—try this.
The ten-year vintage Peace. Take a taste.

DIKAIOPOLIS

Uncorking, sniffing, and making a wry face.

                Ugh. This has
the stink of top-level conferences. It's turned sour,
just like our Allies.

OLYMPOS

Holding out a huge bottle.

                Very well, try this:
a thirty-year vintage Peace on land and sea.

DIKAIOPOLIS

*Uncorking and sniffing, then sniffing again incredulously,
then tasting, then tasting again and breaking into a broad smile.*

Festival of Bacchos! The true bouquet of bliss!
This has the aroma of nectar, the whiff of ambrosia,
I taste the end of forced marches and short rations,
and in my mouth the wine sets up a chant:
Goodbye to Regimentation!
                This is mine!
For drink and sacrifice, this is the wine I choose!
And for the Acharnians—a long farewell from me.
My war is over, my distress is done!
I'll celebrate the Feast of Dionysos,
God of Wine,

Holding up the bottle.

           and now the God of Peace.

OLYMPOS

And, as for me, I'll run away from the Acharnians.

*Both exit, Olympos off-stage as fast as he can, Dikaiopolis
slowly and luxuriously into his house.*

After a short pause, the Chorus enters, wheezing and puffing in
slow and painful pursuit, led by the First and Second Koryphaioi.
They are dressed in long, ragged cloaks, and represent aged charcoal-burners
from the Athenian deme of Acharnai. The scene is understood
to have shifted from the Pnyx to the environs of Dikaiopolis'
house, outside the walls of Athens.

FIRST KORYPHAIOS

This way, men! Over here! Follow him—track him down!
Sound out everybody you meet! Trapping the traitor
is a Civic Duty—

      Athens Expects, and all that.

To the audience.

      —Pardon,

but is there anyone in the house who can possibly give us
some information? Did a man run through here recently, holding
(excuse the word) a TRUCE? And if so, which way did he go?

FIRST SEMICHORUS

Woe—he has vanished! Woe—he has fled!
Woe for my own decrepitude!
Woe for my youth, for the thews which knew
to shrug a burden and run to a draw
PHAŸLLOS the fleet.* If Then were Now,
this scum with the treaty wouldn't escape
and swirl with scornful ease from my grip:
    If Now were Then,
    I'd run him down!

SECOND KORYPHAIOS

But it's Now, not Then. Be realistic, men—just look at us:
I've pulled up lame already; old Lakrateides' legs
are practically ossified. But still, let's not give up the chase!
It's a Question of Honor: We may be doddering, decrepit, ramshackle—
But we're ACHARNIANS first, by god! If he gets away, it's Disgrace—
our proud name ground in the dust by the heel of a light-foot Traitor!

SECOND SEMICHORUS

Damn him, O Zeus and Gods on high!
Damn his truce! But especially
damn the SPARTANS forevermore!
They left my fields dead and sere,
they razed my grapes—and they'll reap WAR!
I'll stick and stake them! I'll thrust and pierce
right up to the stock—and never cease
    till the last one refrains
    from trampling my vines!

FIRST KORYPHAIOS

First things first. Later, the War; Now, the Traitor.
Stalk him, dog him, ferret him out! Ransack the world!
And leave no stone unturned—he might have crawled underneath.
If not, take the stone along and throw it when we find him.

DIKAIOPOLIS

From within his house.

LET EVERYONE KEEP HOLY SILENCE!

SECOND KORYPHAIOS

Be still, everybody! Didn't you hear that call for silence?
This is the fellow we're looking for!—Look, out of the way!
I think our man is coming outside here to sacrifice.

*The Chorus retires to the right. Dikaiopolis emerges from his house,
carrying a pot. He is followed by his daughter, who carries a basket
containing the offerings; his wife; and two slaves, who bear
a huge phallus on a pole.*

DIKAIOPOLIS

LET EVERYONE KEEP HOLY SILENCE!

He surveys his group.

The basket bearer should move up front just a bit.

His daughter moves slightly forward.

And Xanthias ought to set up the Phallus.

Xanthias and the other slave wrestle the phallus into an erect position.

—Daughter,
put down the basket, and we'll begin the rite.

DAUGHTER

Mother, hand me the ladle. It's time to pour
the sauce over the cake.

She does so. Dikaiopolis gives his entourage a last inspection.

DIKAIOPOLIS

Excellent!

He prays.

O Lord Dionysos,
Let this procession and this solemn sacrifice we make
find favor in your eyes. May I and all my household
conduct once more the country festival by which
we honor you as God of Growth and Increase.
Once again let us celebrate the Country Dionysia.*
Grant, O Lord, your blessings now on me,
freed from the army's service and returned to yours.
And let this Peace of Thirty Years endure,
and bring us health, wealth, and true happiness.

Amen.

He turns to his daughter. He is obviously somewhat distressed by her ragged, not-too-clean clothing (a condition which she shares with the rest of the family; Peace has come to Dikaiopolis, but Prosperity has not) and her gawky adolescence. He conceals the distress from her, but not from the audience.

> Daughter dear, you have an important role
> in a most holy rite: you're bearing the basket for Bacchos.
> So be correct and proper. Look demure. Dainty. Sweet.

The daughter tries. He shudders, and speaks in a disgusted aside.

Did I say sweet? Sweet as vinegar!
                    That's perfect, darling.

It'll be a lucky man who marries you, it will!
You'll breed him a lovely tribe—polecats, probably—
just like their mother—farting away in the wee hours.
The dawn comes up like thunder, so does she.
Move on, dear, but careful—someone in that crowd

He gestures at the empty stage.

might sneak up in the confusion and nibble off
all these jewels.

He points to the audience.

Watch out for *that* mob, too.

To the slaves, who have set the phallus down.

Xanthias, you know what this is? It's a phallic procession.
This is the Phallus, the Symbol of Phales, the god.

He indicates his daughter.

And *that* is the basket bearer, the Ritual Virgin.
Now, the two of you get in behind that Virgin
and erect that Symbol—and keep it erect.

Don't droop!
I'll bring up the rear and sing the Phallic Hymn.

To his wife.

Get a good seat, dear—watch from the roof.

His wife disappears into the house, to reappear a moment later on the roof.

For-*ward!*

*The procession makes a slow circuit of the stage, in time with Dikaiopolis'
singing of the hymn to the personified phallus, Phales.*

O Phales, Bacchos' fellow, friend,
carouser, king of guests,
night-wanderer, adulterer—
Holy one, O Pederast!
O Phales, Phales, favor our feast.

I greet you after six years, Lord.
Gone beyond recall
are war neuroses and Lamachóses;
my shield hangs on the wall.
O Phales, Phales, favor our feast.

My night patrols are sweeter now:
I guard against the raids
and forays on my firewood, led
by sexy serving-maids.

When one comes jouncing down the hill
with faggots in her hand,
the Larceny is petty—but
the Penalty is grand!

I mount a sudden flank attack,
and take her by surprise,
I enfilade her vineyard, then
de-grape her, Spartanwise!
O Phales, Phales, favor our feast.

O Phales, enter in to us,
and join us in our songs!
Come share our drink, and spread our joy!
Stay up to hail the dawn!

And when the rout is over, Lord,
and all the songs are sung,
a cup of Peace to clear the head—
and only the shield stays hung!
O Phales, Phales, favor our feast.

*The Chorus bursts from concealment and rushes upon the procession.
The daughter and the slaves escape into the house, and the wife
disappears inside from the roof, leaving Dikaiopolis, hugging his pot,
to confront a shower of stones, not too accurately thrown,
from the angry Acharnians.*

FIRST KORYPHAIOS
That's the man! That's the man! Slash him! Smash him!

SECOND KORYPHAIOS
That's the scoundrel. That's the traitor! Rush him! Crush him!

DIKAIOPOLIS
Holy Herakles, what's this? Look out, you'll smash the pot!

FIRST KORYPHAIOS
You're the one we'll crush to death, you rotten renegade!

DIKAIOPOLIS
Unperturbed.
Would you mind disclosing the nature of the charge, reverend
Acharians?

FIRST KORYPHAIOS
What a question! You've got no shame—and you'll get no pity!

27

You betrayed the City—YOU MADE A TRUCE ON YOUR OWN!
  And still
you have the gall to look Athenians like us in the eye!

DIKAIOPOLIS
I admit it. I made a truce—but I had reasons. Listen.
FIRST KORYPHAIOS
Listen to *you?* You listen to *me:* We're entombing you *now!*

DIKAIOPOLIS
Not before you hear me, friends. Please let me speak.

FIRST SEMICHORUS
Gyrating menacingly.

> We refuse! We'd sooner hear Kleon—
> till now, the height of our hates.
> And *him* we plan to flay and tan
> and make into shoes for the Knights!

FIRST KORYPHAIOS
Nothing can change the facts. You made a Truce with the SPARTANS!
We don't want orations—we don't want harangues—WE WANT
  VENGEANCE!

DIKAIOPOLIS
Your singleness of purpose is praiseworthy, Sirs—but scarcely relevant.
Don't stumble over the Spartans—they're peripheral. The question
is the Peace. Hear me, and decide: did I do a Good Thing?

SECOND KORYPHAIOS
GOOD THING? A Truce with SPARTANS? How can you trust
  them? They swear
by adulterated altars, diluted libations, and hollow handshakes!
GOOD THING!

DIKAIOPOLIS
               This is madness, friends. I know the Spartans, too,
and the fact remains that they're not to blame for all our troubles.

FIRST KORYPHAIOS
NOT ALL! You've compounded your treason; this is Patent Betrayal!
  NO QUARTER!

DIKAIOPOLIS
I repeat: *The Spartans are not to blame for all our troubles.*
Why, I, as I stand before you now, could point out a sizable
number of complaints that the Spartans have against us, complaints
that are well-authenticated and, more important, perfectly reasonable.

SECOND KORYPHAIOS

Staggering, hand to chest.

Sorry, men—my heart can't stand shock the way it used to.
I never heard the like!—You mean you'll defend the ENEMY? HERE?
TO US?

DIKAIOPOLIS

Since you put it that way, yes.

With a wave at the audience.

And such is the power of Truth
on the sovereign people of Athens, that I feel little or no
hesitation at offering to address this crowd like What's-his-name
in Euripides' play.

SECOND KORYPHAIOS

What play?

DIKAIOPOLIS

I forget. But the name doesn't matter.
It's the *mise en scène,* the stark, tragic alternatives:

Victory

or Death—in this case, Persuasion or Decapitation. I'll speak with my
head . . .

SECOND KORYPHAIOS

Eagerly.

On the Block?

DIKAIOPOLIS

No, this is still a Comedy—with my head on the
Breadboard.*

FIRST KORYPHAIOS

Resolute as ever, to the Chorus.

Townsmen, neighbors, up and at him! Fling those stones!
Outfit this turncoat properly—dress him in Spartan colors:
rich, shiny, sticky, gooey, bloody RED!

DIKAIOPOLIS

As the Chorus, with wild shouts, advances again.

What have we here—another flare-up? I swear, you men
have clinkers for hearts. Occupational hazard, I imagine.

The brandishings become more violent.

Hmmm.

I take it, members of the Ancient & Noble Order of the Sons
of Acharnai, that, deep down, you don't prefer to hear my speech?

FIRST KORYPHAIOS

Never!

DIKAIOPOLIS
Is this final?

FIRST KORYPHAIOS
NEVER!—I mean, yes—it's final.

DIKAIOPOLIS
That's really too bad.

SECOND KORYPHAIOS
We'll die before we listen to you!

DIKAIOPOLIS
I suppose you might. But don't on my account, Brothers of the Benevolent
& Protective Association of Aged Acharnian Heroes.

FIRST KORYPHAIOS
TRAITOR,
YOU DIE!

He raises a rock. The Chorus follows suit.

DIKAIOPOLIS
Now, look here, Gentlemen, this has gone far enough!
This brawling and backbiting is simply too much, and I hereby serve notice
that I intend to bite back. "Die," you say, do you?
Well, it's Death for Death—REPRISALS, Gentlemen!
I hold as hostages
your most adored, your dearest friends and relatives—the which
I now shall flay and disembowel before your horrified gaze.

He turns on his heel and enters his house.

SECOND KORYPHAIOS
Men of Acharnai, neighbors, what could he mean? Do you think
he has one of our children penned up inside his house?

FIRST KORYPHAIOS
Impossible!

SECOND KORYPHAIOS
That may be so, but where do you suppose he gets
his confidence?

*Dikaiopolis returns and stands before his door. In his left hand
is a large scuttle full of charcoal; in his right, a huge carving knife.
The Chorus recoils in horror.*

DIKAIOPOLIS
Very well, Sirs—stone if you must. But a word of warning:

One pebble in my direction, and I'll destroy this scuttle
and its defenseless contents.

                  Any charcoal-lovers* present?

He raises the knife.

                                          By god,
I'll find out soon enough.

CHORUS

              —No! No! Not that!
—I can't bear to look!
              —I'll die!
                    —That scuttle's a schoolmate!
  A neighbor!
—An old and valued family friend!
                    —No, please! I beg you!
—I implore you, whatever you do, DON'T!
                —NO!
                  —NO!

DIKAIOPOLIS
Gentlemen, your little friends are doomed. Those howls and pleas
are futile—I refuse to listen.

SECOND KORYPHAIOS

              Can't you reconsider, Sir?
Does Friendship, tried in the furnace, mean nothing at all to you?

FIRST KORYPHAIOS
Can't you see that even a lump of carbon has feelings?

DIKAIOPOLIS
Why should I listen to you? Did you listen to me?

SECOND KORYPHAIOS

                      Then speak!
Give us ALL the particulars, here and now!

FIRST KORYPHAIOS

                    There's nothing
we crave to hear so much as a good pro-Spartan speech!

SECOND KORYPHAIOS
It may mean nausea, cramps, and heartbreak—but I won't betray that
    scuttle.

DIKAIOPOLIS
    All right—but show good faith. Shake the rocks out of your cloaks.

The members of the Chorus shake their cloaks violently.
A clatter of rocks to the ground.

SECOND KORYPHAIOS

There they are, Sir. And now, Fair Play. Put that sword away.

DIKAIOPOLIS

I still have my doubts. Not that I don't trust you, of course,
but one or two rocks might still be lurking in your folds.

SECOND SEMICHORUS

Gyrating desperately, flapping their cloaks.

> We've shaken them out—not a pebble!
> We are, Sir, de-lapidated.
> So keep your word, and put up your sword,
> and commence your defense, as stated.

Retaining the scuttle, Dikaiopolis puts the carving knife down.
A sigh of relief from the Chorus.

DIKAIOPOLIS

Saved—from disaster scarcely a stone's throw distant,
Gentlemen. No thanks to you. You were ready to rock me
with your war cry, and thus ensure the death of Your Own—
these poor coals from Parnes, mute martyrs
to their comrades' monomania.

> Gaze at this pitiful scuttle,
still quivering and distraught! At your attack, black fear
clutched at its vitals—and squeezed. Squidlike, it squirted
an entire peck of coal dust over me—its Savior.
Gentlemen, I ask you: *Aren't you ashamed of yourselves?*
Look at you: Men?

> MUST! Venerable verjuice—
raw wine in rotted bottles, stopped forever
against the infusion of Opposing Views, Fair Play,
or Common Sense.

> Case in point—the Present.
You burst your seams, and spray your howls and stones,
while here I stand, willing to expose my every
last pro-Spartan argument from the Breadboard. Did *I*
give in to passion, or madness, or pique? And yet
I swear I love my life no less than you.

FIRST SEMICHORUS

> We must protest your reticence:
> We're aching for your eloquence,
> and beg you, in all deference,
> to put aside your diffidence
> and bring your Breadboard out—
> AND SPEAK, YOU LOUT!

FIRST KORYPHAIOS

Observe the rules you made—remember? Persuasion
or Decapitation? Now set up that Board of Inquiry and commence.

*Carrying the scuttle, Dikaiopolis enters his house, to emerge in
a moment staggering under the weight of a huge breadboard. This
he places prominently before the house.*

DIKAIOPOLIS

Proceed with your inspection, Gentlemen. I trust that everything
will meet your specifications. Over here, the Breadboard.
—And here, unaccustomed as I am . . .
                                        You have reservations?
Rest assured, Gentlemen, that I have none. Observe:
nothing up my sleeve, no concealed shields, breastplates,
bucklers, cuirasses—or mental blocks. My defense
of Sparta will not be buttressed with qualifications, or hedged
about with Significant Omissions. I shall speak the truth
as I see it, unarmed and steady as a rock . . .
                                        in fact,
Petrified. Know Your Enemy, they say. Well,
I Know My Audience (which, in this case, is the same thing),
and Knowledge is Terror. Look at them:
                                        First, the Farmers,
up from the country for the day. A happy breed—
too happy. Wafted into mindless bliss by any
flag-waving, any patriotic puff from a charlatan,
and to hell with the facts—their country, right or wrong—
true Slaves of the Laud. Their price is praise. They're bought
and sold by demagogues, and never know it.

Pointing at another section of the audience.

                                        Next, mark
the Gaffers—crabbed old men who gum their gruel
and long but to bite again—and, possessed of nothing
sharp but their convictions, enroll as jurors
and convict, over and over, in merciless mastication.

Pointing at another section of the audience very specifically.

And Kleon.*
                Him I know from—shall we say?—
personal experience. Last year's comedy provoked him.
To say the least. He dragged me into the Senate House,
sued me, and opened the sluicegates. Slander and lies
gushed from his tongue in torrents, and down the arroyo
of his mind there roared a flash flood of abuse. To purge me,

he purged himself—and in the offal, filth, and fetor
of his verbal diarrhea, I nearly smothered, mortally
immerded.

To himself.

But wait. They're all Athenians, and every
Athenian responds nobly to the Appeal to Poverty.
That's IT! I'll dress in wretched rags, in pitiful
patches—the picture of a beggar!

—May I have your permission,
Gentlemen, to retire for a moment and change my costume?

SECOND SEMICHORUS
We feel this oversubtlety
must indicate anxiety.
Thus we, in all humility,
suggest invisibility,
or some such folderol—
BUT HURRY—DON'T STALL!

SECOND KORYPHAIOS
Go change. And be as clever as you like. But remember:
There is no delay allowed in this debate!

The Chorus retires to the right, leaving Dikaiopolis alone.

DIKAIOPOLIS
Now, if ever, must I assume a Hero's
Soul . . . But where to get hold of one? And where
to find those rags, for that matter? Let's see . . .

Of course!
There's only one source of supply:
EURIPIDES!
It's obvious—
he produces the rattiest heroes in town.

*He strides purposefully to Euripides' house, center, and
bangs on the door.*

Porter!

KEPHISOPHON*
Opening the door and peering out lugubriously.
Whence is that knocking?

DIKAIOPOLIS
Hello. Is Euripides in?

KEPHISOPHON
Within, he is without—if you have the wit
to conceive me.

DIKAIOPOLIS
I can't even understand you. You say
he's *in* and *not* in?

KEPHISOPHON

      Precisely, Reverend Sir.
It's a paradox—the exegesis is really quite elementary:
His mind is *out*side, culling floscules of fustian,
bouquets of lays and poesies—while he himself
is *in*side, feet up, composing a tragedy in well-wrought
earnest. He has, in short, achieved Dissociation
of Sensibility.

DIKAIOPOLIS

     Ah, Euripides, happiest of dramatists!
Did ever such a subtle servant exist in nature?
What other playwright has philosophers for slaves?

            —Very well,
summon him out.

KEPHISOPHON

     But that's impossible!

DIKAIOPOLIS

        Notwithstanding,
summon him anyway.

Kephisophon retreats inside with a sniff and slams the door.

      No matter. You won't get rid of me—
I'll batter the door. Down, if I have to.

He bangs on the door, shouting.

        EURIPIDES!

No answer.

  YOO-HOO, EURIPIDES!

No answer. He stops knocking.

     No use. How *do* you call
a tragedian to the door?

      Of course!

Tragically.

       *If e'er you hearkened
to mortal in torment, Euripides, hearken now,
I pray you, to me, Dikaiopolis—blasted from birth.*

*He taps lightly. The double doors spring open at his touch, exposing
Euripides' study, which rather resembles a junk shop. The floor
is littered with oddments, mostly receptacles in various stages of
disrepair, while all about the walls is hung and piled a profusion
of impossibly ragged cloaks and hats. Euripides himself is reclining,
facing the audience, on a couch which resembles a chaise longue.
He is meditating vacuously, tablet and stylus in hand. Kephisophon
stands at the head of couch with tablet and stylus, imitating his
master in every particular. Both look up, annoyed, at the interruption.*

36

EURIPIDES

Hence, pest! I'm busy.

DIKAIOPOLIS

                    Have the stagehands wheel
your set out here.

EURIPIDES

          But that's impossible!

DIKAIOPOLIS

                         Notwithstanding,
have them do it anyway.

EURIPIDES

             Very well. They may wheel
me out—

Glancing from the couch to the floor, a distance of about two feet.

        but I have no time to waste in descending.

The set is wheeled forward to the center of the stage.
Dikaiopolis stands by it.

DIKAIOPOLIS
EURIPIDES!

EURIPIDES
Why this vociferous apostrophe?

DIKAIOPOLIS
Normally,
they tell me, people write with their feet on the ground.
But yours don't touch it.
—No wonder your heroes are cripples!
And why in the world are you dressed in those miserable, filthy
tragic rags?
No wonder your heroes are beggars!

To himself.
Heroes? Beggars? I almost forgot.

To Euripides.
In my need,
I implore you by your knees.

He kneels by the couch and tries to clasp the tragedian around
his legs, an undertaking quite distasteful to Euripides, who
keeps struggling to disentangle himself.

O Knees of Euripides,
vouchsafe me a tatter or two from that threadbare tragedy
of yours. You see, I have to make a lengthy formal
defense to the Chorus, and I absolutely must persuade them:
I either turn their heads, or lose my own.

EURIPIDES
You wish rags, eh?

DIKAIOPOLIS
Yes, rags.

EURIPIDES
Have you a preference?

He gestures at the accumulation of ragged clothes.

DIKAIOPOLIS
Er—yes . . .

EURIPIDES
Specifically, then, which rags?—Confused, eh?

Pointing to a set of rags. At each successive name, he indicates another.

Do these
strike a chord? My best. Monuments to misery.
Oineus wore them—you remember the play, of course.

DIKAIOPOLIS
No, not Oineus. It was someone even more miserable.

EURIPIDES
Poor, blind Phoinix, perchance?

DIKAIOPOLIS
No, not Phoinix.
It was someone else. Even shabbier than Phoinix.

EURIPIDES
Than Phoinix?—What fouler, more unlovely tatters
could there be?—Perhaps the scraps of Philoktetes the beggar?

DIKAIOPOLIS
No, not him. This Hero beggared all description.

EURIPIDES
Then you must mean this—the loathesome, bedrabbled burlap
worn by Bellerophon the cripple.

DIKAIOPOLIS
No, not Bellerophon.
—First, my Hero was a combination of all those others—
not blind, though. But he *was* a beggar, a cripple, and a windbag:
The Perfect Orator.—Does that help?

EURIPIDES
Proceed.

DIKAIOPOLIS
Let me think.
It's been almost fifteen years . . .
Oh, yes—he wasn't
really a beggar.

EURIPIDES
They never are.

DIKAIOPOLIS
But he dressed
as a beggar in order to make a speech—like me.
He had to convince some Greeks that he wasn't a traitor.
To do this, he had to prove that some war was pointless—
that its cause was some woman or other who wasn't worth it.

EURIPIDES
They never are.
                        —But hold on a minute! Was this
the Trojan War? And Helen?

DIKAIOPOLIS
                        That's right—And he spoke
with his head on a Block—like me—and won over the King.

EURIPIDES
Agamemnon?

DIKAIOPOLIS
                Yes, that was the King—And just when he had
the Greeks convinced, in came a soldier . . .

EURIPIDES
                                        Achilles?

DIKAIOPOLIS
Yes. And . . .

EURIPIDES
                I know! It's . . .

DIKAIOPOLIS
                This soldier upset everything.
He threatened to kill . . .

EURIPIDES
                But I . . .

DIKAIOPOLIS
                                . . . the Beggar—who was really
a King!

EURIPIDES
        It's *The Tragicall* . . .

DIKAIOPOLIS
                But what I forget . . .

EURIPIDES
                                        . . . *Historie* . . .

DIKAIOPOLIS
. . . is how it turned out.

EURIPIDES
                . . . *of Telephos, King of Mysia!*

DIKAIOPOLIS
Telephos! Yes! Oh, to swaddle myself in Telephos'
vile vestments! I supplicate you, Euripides: Please
confer upon me that mighty Hero's clout!

EURIPIDES

I'd love to. So be it.

—Kephisophon, tender him the tatters
of Telephos. You'll find them over there, sandwiched in
between Ino's rags and Thyestes' patchwork.

Kephisophon digs out a particularly loathesome cloak. Euripides
turns to Dikaiopolis.

Behold!
O happy man, since even now the object
of all your desire shudders expectant for your grasp!
Take, and, taking, love these shoddy shreds!

DIKAIOPOLIS

Taking the cloak, lifting it up, and peering through the numerous holes.

O Zeus, whose holy gaze does pierce and penetrate
through all our mortal raiment to the shuddering clay
beneath, grant that I may now be garbed
most grievously, in the world's most woebegone weeds.

He puts the cloak on, then holds it wide before Euripides.

Euripides, the breadth of your generosity is justly vaunted—

Shaking the perforated folds of the cloak.

not to say vented—and such beneficence, I am sure,
would never knowingly be left unfinished. I beg you,
cap this kindness, Sir: Bestow upon me
the appropriate, matching props—but, most of all,

Pointing.

that little Mysian bonnet to shroud my head.

Striking a tragic attitude.

This very day must I a mendicant mime,
must be the thing I am, yet seem another.
The audience, of course, is sure to know who I am—
but the Chorus must stand there stupefied, a flock of fools
for me to twit and twiddle with tragic ironies.

EURIPIDES

I accede.

He motions to Kephisophon, who procures the bonnet and gives it
to Dikaiopolis. This sequence of events is repeated with subsequent items,
the basket excepted.

I do endorse and approbate, Sir,
your torturous, twisted plots, the protean offspring
of a mind thick-packed with thin-drawn strands of craft.

DIKAIOPOLIS

Putting the bonnet on, then taking it off in a sweeping bow.

Fortune attend you, Sir,—and, as for Telephos,
may that which I intend attend him:

In a loud mock-aside.

Fairer
Fortune, for Telephos is I, and I am Telephos.
—Say, that's not bad! Do the quotes come along with the cloak?
—However, Sir, my need is still a great one:
My guise literally cries for a beggar's staff.

EURIPIDES

Take it.
And now, Sir, hie thee hence, from out
this vaulted marble pile.

DIKAIOPOLIS

To himself, loudly.

Alas, my Soul,*
dost see how I am scorned and thrust away
though yet in grating need of tragic trash?
Come, be importunate, Soul: Increase your appeals!
Expand your prayers! Broaden your orisons!

—Euripides,
please fetch from your treasures a trifle for an indigent beggar?—
A tiny, battered, burned, and broken basket?

EURIPIDES

What need hath wrought within thy soul this wish
for wicker, wretch?

DIKAIOPOLIS

Who *needs* it? I just *want* it.

EURIPIDES

Snatching the basket from Kephisophon and throwing it at Dikaiopolis.

Look, you bother me. Now, dammit, GET OUT!

DIKAIOPOLIS

Alas!

Fortune attend thee, and mayst thou grow in grace
as well as e'er thy mother did—in groceries*

EURIPIDES

Dammit, LEAVE ME ALONE!

DIKAIOPOLIS

Just one more thing?—
A lopsided, misfired mug that's chipped on the lip?

EURIPIDES

Take it to perdition, damn you!
                                    And be apprised
that you do sorely vex and gall our halls!

DIKAIOPOLIS

Have you ever sat through one of your own tragedies?

Talk about pure, unadulterated pestilence!
                                    —Euripides,
sweet, *generous* Friend to All, I make this solitary
request, just this:
                    A teeny pot, a pottie,
please, and a sponge to go with it?

EURIPIDES

                                    Sponge is right!
Do you want to wipe me out?

DIKAIOPOLIS

                                    No, *me*—We beggars
are cleanly where it doesn't show, you know.

EURIPIDES

                                    But this
is horrible—you're stealing my whole tragedy!
                                    —All right,
take it, and, for god's sake, LEAVE!

DIKAIOPOLIS

                                    I *am* leaving—
but whither? I lack the *sine qua non*—without it,
Dikaiopolis is dead!
                    —Euripides, prince of philanthropists,
grant this boon and I shall quit you forever:
Place in the basket a handful of withered leaves
to make my wretched breakfast, lest I die.

EURIPIDES

Die? You'll be the death of *me:* You've beggared
my repertory, looted my dramaturgy—MY PLAYS ARE GONE!

DIKAIOPOLIS

And so am I. I beg no more. I go.
I am become a noisome nuisance in the nostrils
of royal men, unknowing that lords do loathe me.

He turns, takes a step, then turns back.

Oh, NO! Oh, LOST!

I have forgot the hingepin

of my hope, the plinth of all my expectation!
—Euripides, epitome of magnanimity, seraph of sweet
charity, Good Guy *sans peur et sans reproche*—
may I be dissolved beyond redemption, if ever
I make petition more, beyond this lonely,
onliest request: *Give me thy mother's legacy:*
A pound and a half of wilted water cress?

EURIPIDES
Livid, to Kephisophon.

This man mouths insolence! Ho, occlude the portcullis!
Kephisophon pushing, the set is drawn back to its original position.
The doors shut with a crash, and Dikaiopolis is left alone.

DIKAIOPOLIS

O rash! O hasty! O most ungenerous! O crass!
—Ah, Soul, we must fare away without the cress.
Soul of my Soul, do you know what shortly awaits you?
The dread debate which you must make on behalf
of SPARTA?

—O my Soul, I'm glad I'm not *you!*

He draws an imaginary line in front of him with the beggar's staff.

Behold the starting line. And now, Get Ready—
Get Set—and GO, my swiftly coursing Soul!
He takes three or four brisk steps, then stops, slumping.

What's this? You *stop?* You swallow Euripides whole
and STOP?

O brave! Up, up, my enduring Heart!

Patience! Fortitude! Speed to the goal, O Soul!
He points to the Breadboard before his door.

Take up your stand, and speak, and speak the truth,
and then, unflinchingly, present your head to the dreadful
Breadboard.

Courage! Show some backbone, Heart!

Forward . . . MARCH!—Attaboy, O my Soul!
He sets off manfully for the Breadboard. Reaching it, he leans on it in
elaborate unconcern, to the great surprise of the returning Chorus.

CHORUS
Singly, to Dikaiopolis.

—What can you do?

—What can you say?

—You're an alloy of iron and brass!
—The stake is your head,

—you're only one man,

—you're attacking Athens *en masse!*
        —Look, he doesn't shiver.
            —Not a quiver.
            —No shriek.
    —All right, you wanted it, Hero.
            —Now speak.

DIKAIOPOLIS
Gentlemen of the audience, I humbly ask your indulgence.
I am cognizant of my audacity: the mere appearance in a Comedy
of that tried-and-true *Tragic* staple, THE BEGGAR,
is sufficient to offend your sense of things-as-they-are.
But when said Beggar, in said Comedy, presumes to lecture
Athenian citizens on the welfare of their State,
outraged traditionalism is far too mild
a reaction to hope for.
                    And yet, my friends, bear with me.
Even Comedy is no stranger to justice, simple
morality, and truth; and though my ensuing remarks
may cause discomfort, irritation, and even pain,
they will undeniably be just, and moral, and true.

The further to ease your minds, I note in passing
that we are, so to speak, in closed session here.
A year ago, Kleon charged that I had slandered
the State in the presence of strangers, by presenting my play,
The Babylonians, at our Great Festival of Dionysos.
I do not admit the truth of this charge even now,
but I point out that it cannot apply to the present:
This is the Lenaia*—our personal, private feast—
Athenians Only; Foreigners Please Keep Out—
and neither troops nor tribute have yet arrived
from our Noble Allies. The whole great harvest of Empire
is winnowed, the chaff and straw are scattered abroad,
and only the citizens of Athens, the fine kernels
of grain, remain.
                    —Not to forget, of course,
our Loyal Resident Aliens, whom, in completion
of a metaphor, I might term the nourishing bran.
My criticisms, then, are strictly *entre nous.*

Gentlemen, I am, have been, and always will be
a Spartan-hater. I loathe Spartans. I detest
Spartans. I abominate Spartans. In vengeance
for my darling vineyards, by the fell SPARTAN'S hand
untimely cropt—even as yours—I here

implore Poseidon the Earthshaker, god of Tainaros,
to shake, quake, shiver, and tumble their hovels
into rubble, to rain destruction on those damnable animals!

Changing tone completely.

But they're only human, and we're too hard on them, friends.
Why should we blame the Spartans for all our troubles?
Specifically, the War? The cause, if the truth were known,
was our own people—
                  Note, I do not say Athens.
Particularly note, Gentlemen, that I do *not* say
Athens.—
              It was our own men, a few corrupt men,
debased, mis-struck types, the bastard pinchbeck outpouring
of foreign mints, the all-too-common coins,
the Two-Bit Informers—the Co. of Kleon & Co.
It was they who denounced and reported as illegal the entry
of those little jackets they make over in Megara.
It was they who extended the rubric, PROHIBITED IMPORT,
to cover Megara's entire annual output.
It was they who glued their beady eyes to the Customs,
and, at first sight of a cucumber, a rabbit, a pig,
even a clove of garlic or a lump of salt,
bawled out, "MEGARIAN CONTRABAND!"—saw to confiscation,
and pocketed a fat percentage.
                 These matters were minimal,
purely domestic in their impact: Megara *did* have
other markets. Nevertheless, the stage
was set, and the required International Incident
followed shortly. Certain of the Youth of Athens—
Our Greatest Resource, Gentlemen, Our Hope for the Future—
got sloppy drunk at chug-a-lug, reeled over to Megara,
and carried off a Megarian whore.—
                     OUTRAGE!
DISGRACE! DISHONOR! And every Megarian hackle
went stiff with pride and vengeance. Reprisal was swift:
They abducted *two* whores from Aspasia's stable in Athens.
And the whirlwind of War burgeoned and burst on all Greece
simply to answer the question: WHO STOLE THE TARTS?
For Olympian Perikles, godlike in his wrath—and Aspasia's—
thundered and lightninged, wholly embrangling Hellas
with laws that read like nothing so much in the world
as drinking songs:

We hereby decree
that Megara be
placed under embargo.
Her cargo is consequently banned
from every market, from land,
from sea, and—
should the occasion arise—
from the skies.*

The Megarians, thus cut off from trade, replied
to our blockade by starving, slowly and painfully,
until they were reduced to applying to Sparta
for aid and assistance. They beseeched them, as fellow Dorians,
to press for a reversal of the Three-Prostitute-Statute.
No use. To all petitions and representations,
however reasonable, we returned one answer—
                                        NO.
And that's how, and when, and why the Spartans started
to rattle their sabers.
                          I sense an objection here.
Some one of you may say the offense, if offense it was,
was slight, and nothing to go to war about.
I can hear it now: "The Spartans' action was immoral!"
But what alternatives had they? Try the situation
on yourselves for size.
                          Put the case that some Spartan
sailed out in a rowboat to our most godforsaken island,
laid hold of the mangiest, scrawniest fleabag of a dog
in the place, and confiscated same.
                                    What would *you* do?
Sit quietly at home?
                    Not a chance.
                                  You'd launch immediately
a fighting fleet of some three hundred ships
and fill the whole city with martial hullabaloo:
caterwauling soldiers shouting "Captain!"
the slosh of gilt on figureheads, the brays
for wages, market-racket, ration-ruckus,
wineskins, warwhoops, oarloops, pots for sale
and *smash!*—
              the crush for garlics, olives, onions,
chaplets,
        chops,
              flutists,
                      fist-fights,
                                black eyes.

While down at the docks it's bolts and jolts and spars
and oars, roars, planes, thongs, bongs,
and fifes,
      fracas,
          bos'ns,
               pipes,
                    and tweets.
Put it all together, it spells CHAOS—
or War in Self-Defense, it's generally known.
And that, my friends, is precisely the way you'd act.
It's precisely the way the Spartans *did* act.
                        And if
you think anyone, even a Euripidean hero,
even Telephos, would behave in any other fashion,
you've no damn sense—
                which is not, of course, unlikely.

FIRST KORYPHAIOS
So? You sly, sneaky insinuator of sedition!
Your logic is looser than your morals. An informer or two
in town makes US guilty of aggression?—TREASON!

SECOND KORYPHAIOS
To the First Koryphaios.

Hold on; are you sure you heard him? That's not Treason!
He's right; he convinced ME! Every word of that speech
was Just! Also Moral! Not to forget True!

FIRST KORYPHAIOS
Justice be damned! Ditto Morality! Truth, too!
Anyway, who's HE to talk? Treason or not,
it's Insolence—which is worse! He won't get away with THAT!

*The First Semichorus makes for Dikaiopolis, but is stopped by the
Second, the members of which interpose themselves in the path
of the attack.*

SECOND KORYPHAIOS
Not so fast—what's your hurry? HANDS OFF!
For every finger you lay on him, you lose two!

*A brawl ensues between the two Semichoruses, in which the First
(the anti-Dikaiopolitans) gets considerably the worst of it.
They turn to the house of Lamachos, right, and call for help.*

> Torn with travail,
> hemmed in, and harassed,
> we summon and hail
> that sterling militarist
> MAJOR LAMACHOS
> to rescue us.
> HELP! FRIEND LAMACHOS! HELP!

Since no help seems forthcoming from Lamachos' house, and the Second Semichorus is increasing its advantage, they turn desperately to the audience.

> We appeal to *you.*
> Would a General, if requested,
> or a Captain, *faute de mieux,*
> or even an Enlisted
> Man deliver us!
> They'll murder us!
> HELP! PLEASE, ANYBODY! HELP!

There is a loud, gaudy fanfare. The fight stops, never to be resumed, and the Semichoruses turn expectantly toward Lamachos' house, where the door is opening. A pause. Then the fanfare is heard again. A second pause, just slightly too long. Lamachos strides through his door and stands before it, surveying the stage. He is in full armor, wears a long cloak, and bears a considerable amount of ordnance, including a shield with a huge Gorgon emblazoned upon it, a sword, and two lances. These trappings are not realistic, but visual parodies, violent exaggerations. Most noteworthy is the helmet: various feathers are affixed to its cheekpieces, and it is capped by, not one, but three huge, brilliantly dyed horsehair crests.

Lamachos, of course, is the original Miles Gloriosus, and possessed of all the rodomontade, bluster, and boastful bloodthirstiness that pertain to this type. But there is one important difference between him and most of his successors in Western comedy, of whom Falstaff is the best known: Lamachos is a relatively young man, and should be shown as such. *Both his trappings and his rhetoric are much too large for him, and his command of them deserts him frequently, as when he trips on his sword, or fails, for all his fustian, to debate with Dikaiopolis. Dikaiopolis vs. Lamachos should be visually recognizable as Age vs. Youth as well as Peace vs. War. Lamachos need not be presented as a Boy Wonder, but he should be the shortest man on stage.**

LAMACHOS

Who cried Havoc? Who waked the ghastly, grim-visaged
Gorgon from her shield?—I distinctly heard a shout
portending internecine struggle, slaughter, and decimation.
As a qualified patriot, I sped hotfoot to the fray.
—Well, where is it? Where am I to deploy
reinforcements? Where throw up my breastworks?
—You bloody fools—
                    WHAT HAVE YOU DONE WITH THE WAR?

DIKAIOPOLIS

O Lamachos! Hero of Crests and Purple Patches!*

FIRST KORYPHAIOS

That's the fellow, Major, right there! He just finished
slandering Athens! *In toto!* But especially US!

LAMACHOS

Treason?

Muttering as he crosses to Dikaiopolis.
                    Damned civilians.

*Stopping some distance from Dikaiopolis and peering at the
Euripidean outfit.*
                              A beggar, eh?
—You there, you scrubby vulgarian, have you the infernal
effrontery to—

DIKAIOPOLIS

Wheedlingly.

                    Major, *Sir,* a genuine hero
like *you* will certainly pardon a poor old beggarman
for tripping over his tongue once or twice. Please?

LAMACHOS

Don't shilly-shally, man. This treason: What did you say?

DIKAIOPOLIS

I forget—You see, these spells come over me.

LAMACHOS

Spells?

DIKAIOPOLIS

        Vertigo. When I see armor, I'm frightened—
and when I'm frightened, I'm dizzy—and when I'm dizzy, my head
goes round and round and—
                              OOPS—there it goes!

LAMACHOS

                                        What's this?

DIKAIOPOLIS

Pointing to the Gorgon on the shield.

That armor! Oblige an old beggar and hide that goblin?

LAMACHOS

Turning his shield around.

Very well.

DIKAIOPOLIS

No—upside down. Over here.

LAMACHOS

There it is.

DIKAIOPOLIS

Suddenly doubling up.

OWWW!

LAMACHOS

What *now?*

DIKAIOPOLIS

Please, Sir, a plume from your helmet?

LAMACHOS

Very well—but not an entire plume. One feather.

He extracts a huge, gaudy feather from a cheekpiece plume and hands it to Dikaiopolis.

DIKAIOPOLIS

Leaning over the shield.

Now hold my head, please.

Lamachos obeys almost mechanically. Dikaiopolis prepares to tickle his throat with the feather.

Thanks, I have to vomit.
It's those crests—I'm allergic to horsehair.

LAMACHOS

Letting go with a start.

What? Vomit?
By god, you DARE to vomit with LAMACHOS' feather?

DIKAIOPOLIS

Yours, O bird most rare?

What species?—Don't tell me,
let me guess. Could you be the Great-Crested Peewee? No?
the Blabber-Breasted Boastard?

LAMACHOS

Reaching for his sword.

You scurvy canaille,
you die!

*The sword is inextricably twined in his belt. Dikaiopolis
watches his struggles.*

DIKAIOPOLIS

Tut, Lamachos, old man. Out of the question.
Your strength is helpless here.

He flips open Lamachos' cloak, exposing the phallus.

Besides, you're not equipped
for frontal attacks—more for distending the rear.

LAMACHOS

You whoreson beggar, do you DARE address a GENERAL*
in this insolent, unseemly fashion?

DIKAIOPOLIS

Beggar?

He throws off the rags.

I'm a beggar,
am I?

LAMACHOS

Well, what *are* you, then?

DIKAIOPOLIS

I shall tell you.
I am that bird least rare, but unknown to you:
The Honest Citizen. Not the Very Important Person.
Contrast us, Lamachos. Since the War began,
I've been in the ranks, the plainest of private soldiers.
But *you,* my fine feathered friend—since the War began,
you've been in the banks, a commissioned officer—let's say
supercommissioned. Commission Plus Ten Per Cent.

LAMACHOS

I was Duly Elected, Sir—

DIKAIOPOLIS

—by three jibberjabber
whippersnapper mocking birds, camouflaged as a quorum.
That's the sort of flimflam that stuck in my craw
and made me strike this Truce. I looked at the Army
and saw gray-haired old men filling the front lines,

because the strong young hulks—like you—had dodged
enlisted service by a perfectly legal device:
viz., Due Election.

From the city of Athens there poured
a bewildering stream of beardless civil servants—
ambassadors, messengers, attachés, chargés d'affaires—
functionaries with a single function: to save their skins
by scattering to the points of the compass at State expense.
Oh, what a crowd—the crudded cream of Athens:
the scions of bluebloods, robber barons, plutocrats,
First Families fifteen years off the boat from Skythia—
nouveaux riches, anciens riches, just plain Filthy *riches*—
industrial giants, moral pygmies, experts
in public calumny, and specialists in self-abuse . . .
What a comical bunch! And their ridiculous destinations:
Thrace, to chaff with Sitalkes; Chaonia,* where it's always
Open House, to bugger the obliging Natives;
Sicily, to joy-ride from town to silly town
and show off our Navy in the middle of the War—ridiculous
isn't the word! And the pay—three drachmas per day
per man—an absolute howl!—We nearly died laughing.

LAMACHOS
Those men were Duly Elected, Sir—

DIKAIOPOLIS
Of course,
but how much was Due?—I mean, doesn't it seem
a wee bit odd that youngsters like you can manage,
now and forever, a niche in the yearly budget,
while Men, mature Men—say, these Acharnians here—
never get an obol? Observe:
To a member of the Chorus.
Dusty, my friend,
in all your life—and I can see it's been a long one—
have you ever been an envoy, or held *any* paid position
with the State?
Dusty shakes his head. Dikaiopolis turns back to Lamachos.
Never! And yet he's a prudent, frugal
man—a worker—sound as they come.
To other members of the Chorus.
What do *you* say,
Collier?
—Or *you,* Aschmann?
—Or Kendall here?

—Have you ever seen glorious Ekbatana?

They shake their heads. He turns to others.

—Well, Birnham, you?

—Or maybe Stoker?

—Ever have an all-expense tour
of awe-inspiring Chaonia—The Buggery Coast?

They shake their heads.

Never! So much for Virtue and Thrift—Those appointments
go to aristocratic young decadents, spendthrifts, welshers
like friend Lamachos here. Behold Success!

He points dramatically to Lamachos.

Barely yesterday, friends, Lamachos was up to his clavicle
in unpaid dues and debts. He was the type
whose Best Friends *Told*—they touted perfect strangers
away from him. Socially, friends, the man was a Slum—
possessed of all the popularity of used bathwater . . .

LAMACHOS

In DEMOCRACY'S name! Is such corrupt depravity
to be borne? Is such depraved corruption to be brooked?

DIKAIOPOLIS

Certainly not—unless you continue on the payroll.

Lamachos starts for his sword. Dikaiopolis feints a blow at him.
Lamachos jumps back, cowers briefly, then gathers up his weapons,
clutches his cloak about him, and addresses the audience.

LAMACHOS

Attend my Program and Declaration:

I SHALL PROSECUTE THIS WAR.
I SHALL STRIKE DEEP INTO THE SOFT UNDERBELLY OF
THE PELOPONNESIANS.
I SHALL NOT FLAG OR FAIL. I SHALL FIGHT IN SPARTA.
I SHALL FIGHT ON THE SEAS AND OCEANS, I SHALL FIGHT
ON THE FIELDS
AND IN THE STREETS, I SHALL FIGHT IN THE HILLS: I
SHALL NEVER SURRENDER.

He stalks off, tripping over his sword. Dikaiopolis watches him
leave, then turns to the audience.

DIKAIOPOLIS

Attend my Prospectus and Proclamation:

I SHALL INSTITUTE A MARKET.
I SHALL SELL DELIGHTS FOR THE SOFT UNDERBELLY OF
THE PELOPONNESIANS,
THE MEGARIANS, AND THE BOIOTIANS: I SHALL NOT LACK
FOR SALES.

I INVITE THEM TO LEAVE THEIR HILLS, I INVITE THEM TO
    QUIT
THEIR FIELDS, I INVITE THEM TO TRAVERSE THE SEAS
    AND OCEANS.
I SHALL MEET THEM IN THE STREETS AND THERE ENGAGE
    THEM
IN GOOD OLD ATHENIAN TRADE. I SHALL NEVER
    SURRENDER
MY MONOPOLY. THEY MAY TRADE WITH ME—BUT NOT
    WITH LAMACHOS.

He enters his house.

The Semichoruses reunite and hold a brief whispered consultation.
The First Koryphaios advances to address the audience.

FIRST KORYPHAIOS
RESULTS OF THE DEBATE:
                                    FIRST, DIKAIOPOLIS.
                                        SECOND, LAMACHOS.

A RINGING POPULAR ENDORSEMENT OF THE PEACE!
                            —And now, the customary
Choral Interlude.

To the Chorus.
                    Places, men! It's time for the ANAPESTS.*
Off with the cloaks—let's get this atrophied ritual on the road!

The members of the Chorus remove their cloaks and form behind him.
He comes to the front of the stage and makes his formal address
to the audience.

Gentlemen, our Playwright is a modest man. Never in his career
has he written his ego into the script, or prostituted his Parabasis
to declare his genius. But now that genius is under attack.
Before the people of Athens (so notorious for their snap decisions),
his enemies charge that he degrades the City and insults the Populace.
And thus our Poet requests this time to defend his Art
before the people of Athens (so illustrious for their reasoned revisions
of their snap decisions).
                        Our Poet gives his accusers the lie.
He protests that he is a Public Benefactor, instilling in the Body
Politic a healthy resistance to rhetoric. No longer, Gentlemen,
are you ceaselessly victimized by foreign oratory, willingly wallowing,
unthinking and blissful, in flattering unction—wearing a wide-eyed,
slack-jawed gawk as your National Mien. But think back three years
from this Enlightened Present: the Ambassadors from the Federated
    States

came yearly (at least) to fleece you, with a never-fail one-two punch
compounded of Pindaric epithets—and you never caught on. STEP
    ONE:
They'd hail you as VIOLET-WREATHED. And up to the tips of your
    rumps
you shot, panting for more. And more you got—STEP TWO:
O GLISTERING ATHENS! they'd howl. Thus graced with a term
    quite apt
for sardines, you were hooked—and handed over the whole damned city.
But this is all past, thanks to our Poet—our Public Benefactor.

Consider a second benefit. Gentlemen, why do you think
that the Allies keep flocking to town to pay the tribute you exact?
Because they love you? Because they hate money?

               Not in the least.
Because last year, in *The Babylonians,* a Certain Comic Poet
ripped the lid off the relations between Athens and the rest of the
    Federation,
exposing how we democratically democratize our Allies into Complete
    Equality—
with each other, like slaves. So now these Allies are wild to see
this nonpareil among poets with the Courage to Tell the Truth in
    Athens.
And they come—and you get the money.

           This Courage, in fact, is famous
throughout the world, as witness a recent report from Persia:
It seems that the Great King was sounding out a delegation from Sparta,
and asked about the relative strength of their side and ours.
First, of course, he wanted to know which State had the larger
Navy; but THEN he turned to the question of the famous poet
who criticized his own city without mercy. Which side had HIM?
"The men who have been guided by that adviser," he said,
"are necessarily far superior; their decisive victory in the War
is only a matter of time." And *there* is the reason for the Spartans'
recent suit for Peace—AND their demand for Aigina.
They don't give a damn for Aigina *per se;* they only desire
that island in order to appropriate one of its Summer Residents*—
your Fearless, Peerless Poet, ARISTOPHANES. I urge you, Friends,
don't give him up! Don't discard the Voice of Justice!
—Hear now the pledge of the Poet as Teacher.

            His subtle stagecraft
will bear you along to perfect happiness, public and private.
His integrity remains absolute. He will not knuckle, truckle,

hoax, or coax his way into favor. He will not adulterate
the pure matter of his plays with soft soap, bunkum, or grease,
simply to win a prize. His aim is not your applause, or votes,
but your EDIFICATION:

ONWARD AND UPWARD WITH HIS ART!

Hence—and I quote:*

> *Let the crafty* Kleon *forge and frame*
> *each fell, nefarious plot.*
> *My aide is Justice; my adjutant, Right—*
> *I defy such scheming! I'll not*
> *be caught!*—But his charge of perversion and fear
> could lead to arresting ends . . .
> since the versatile Kleon turns tail to our Foes—
> and repeats the maneuver for Friends.

He rejoins his Semichorus, which steps forward to invoke its Muse.

FIRST SEMICHORUS

> Muse of charcoal,
> Muse combustible,
> Muse of Thermogenesis,
> Muse Acharnian,
> Muse of Arson,
> come, inspire your townsmen—us.
>
> Swiftly fly as
> when the bellows
> frees your godhead from the coal,
> when your essence
> sweeps to ovens
> and invades the mackerel,
>
> heats to ardenc-
> y the sárdines
> filletèd in glistering oil,
> then enkindles
> on the griddles
> fervid seethings in the sole—
>
> Thus our singing
> turn to singeing
> sure to scorch and char—and may
> your afflatus,
> Muse, ignite us:
> We have other fish to fry.

—Specifically, YOU, you greathearted guppies! We Long-Time
  Residents
and Senior Citizens have a bone to pick with the City of Athens.
We'd like to point out a slight discrepancy between the glorious
sea-battles we fought for you once, and the treatment you give us now.
WHOSE SIDE DO YOU THINK WE WERE ON?
                           Look at it fairly: what is our
reward for Age, Service, and, *passim*, Saving the State?
TORTURE! You grease the skids under our declining years,
  and slide us
straight into court, to serve as butts for youngsters-at-law—
to supply these tyro shysters with cash and practice, and yourselves
with laughs. Oh, we fill the role admirably. Halt, lame,
deaf, blind, decayed, decrepit—all the eloquence
of worn-out oboe reeds—all outside support, temporal
and divine, lodged in How Firm a Foundation, The Old, Rugged
Crutch. With such as our ample armor, we totter to Court
and stand before the bench to stammer our senile squeaks,
while the wisps of Law curl so thick we fumble, fogbound by Justice.
Enters then our spruce accuser, milk teeth shining
in expectation of Easy Pickings. Swiftly he softens us up
with a hail of insinuations, a mighty barrage of bald accusations,
and attacks at close quarters. He pulverizes poor Tithonos,
and scatters the pieces at random; and the feeble old fossil, tongue-tied
from age as he is, can't collect himself in time to utter
more than a splutter. Which is not enough. He loses, of course.
And is fined. And, sick with shame, staggers off to die. And can't.
Why? Well, hear him tell it to his friends with sobs and wails:
"How can I buy a coffin? My savings all went for that case!"

SECOND SEMICHORUS
              Clock of Water,*
              Courtroom-Meter,
     Hear your drip-drop's dread result:
              Law diluted,
              Honor spotted,
   Right and Justice warped and spoilt.

              See the Veteran:
              Once his sweat ran
     hot and fierce at Marathon;
              now his hopes flow
              cold, through loopholes,
   litigated down the drain.

Once the Persian
inundation
broke before us, checked and dammed;
now the verdict's
swirling vortex
leaves us broken, charged, condemned.

Clock, forswear your
Rain of Error;
let not lawyers, flush and fee'd,
clear their knavery—
claiming every
silver lining has a cloud.

SECOND KORYPHAIOS

Are these soggy proceedings Justice? Consider some dry specificities.
Inspect the demise of THOUKYDIDES:*
                              In the midst of Athens, there lurks
a shifting Skythian desert, a howling wilderness—in short,
a Public Prosecutor. Its name is EUATHLOS. It's the son of that eminent
immigrant, KEPHISODEMOS (no wee wasteland himself)—and recently
engulfed Thoukydides, smothered and choked him with writs and ropes
of sand.
            —I ask you, Gentlemen, was *this* a Just Desert?
I had to wipe away tears of pity at the sight of this aged
hero, statesman, general, wrestler, and purebred Athenian
drawn, flexed, snapped, and unstrung in the hairy paws
of a half-baked, half-breed bowman! When he was still Thoukydides
the Famous, he wouldn't be flexed by anyone—by Demeter,
                                          not even
by Demeter! He'd have gone to the mat with TEN of those worthless
    Euathloses,
and pinned the pack; and then out-bawled, out-bellowed THREE
    THOUSAND
Skythian archers (cousins of Kephisodemos), unslung his bow . . .
with a single shot, he'd have shafted the lot!

He pauses and shrugs.

                              It's useless to plead.
To you, Age Must Be Served—until you run out of subpoenas.
Facing which sleepless prospect, we oldsters propose an addition
to Judicial Procedure: Partition the populace into OLD and YOUNG,
and decree that defendants and plaintiffs belong to the same Division.
The Old Man's prosecutor must himself be Old and toothless;

the Young Man's prosecutor must himself be a compulsive babbler,
a compliant bugger, and a—well, save time: just say ALKIBIADES.*
Impose a fine for failure to comply; then back to the Great
Athenian National Sport—Courtroom Catharsis. Be regular
in elimination:

Purge Age with Age, and Youth with Youth.

*The Chorus divides and moves to the sides of the stage. Dikaiopolis
enters from his house and marks off a large area before the door.*

DIKAIOPOLIS

I herewith fix the boundaries of my place of business
and send abroad a blanket invitation to the citizens
of Megaria, Boiotia, and the Peloponnese.

HURRY ON DOWN

TO DIKAIOPOLIS' FREE BAZAAR! Contract Acceptance
Contingent on Absolute Avoidance of Business with Lamachos.

*He produces a huge paddle.**

I now present my Board of Trade—the pick of a
large panel—well-seasoned, rigid and unbending
in its application of the solitary Rule of Commerce, *viz.:*
THIS IS NOT A BIRD SANCTUARY! ALL STOOL PIGEONS,
    PEEPERS,
MEDDLING NARKS, AND FINKS ARE HEREBY INFORMED:
OFF LIMITS! STAY OUT! THIS MEANS YOU!

—And now

to fetch that enlarged copy of the Treaty and post it
in a conspicuous spot along the Rialto here.

*He enters the house. After a short pause, a poverty-stricken,
emaciated Megarian* enters from the right, carrying a large and
seemingly empty sack. Two Little Girls follow fearfully at a
distance. They look more wretched than he, if possible.*

MEGARIAN

Empohrium of Athens, highes' hope an' deepes'
desiah of all mah people, Ah take this oppuhtunity
t'extend to y'awl a heartfelt Megarian Howdy-Do.
Bah Hermes, God of Profit an' Loss, Ah've missed yo'
like mah deah ole mammy—bless her greedy soul.

He turns to the Little Girls.

—Dahlin daughtuhs, yo' mizzuble offspring of a sire
whom the clutch of circumstance conspires to mold into a bum,
come heah to yo' daddy, an' prepare to take that first
great step to'd the Ultima Thuley of Worldly Wishes—
Ah refer, of co'se, to FOOD.

—Ef'n yo' kin find any.

The Little Girls break into wails. He raises his voice.

> Ah retain the floor, an' Ah request the respeckful attention
> of yo' bellies! Fill 'em with advice, 'n' yo' *may* git vittles.

The Little Girls subside.

> That's bettuh.—Now, heah are the altuhnatives facin' you two.
> Yo' kin eithuh be sold in the mahket, or else go Home . . .
> to expiah in awful agonies of Uttah Stahvation.
> —Which is yo' pleasure, dahlins?

LITTLE GIRLS

> Sell us! Sell us!

MEGARIAN

> A credit to the fam'ly—just what Ah'd say mahself.
> Still, look at you. Ah shuddah to say it of mah own
> flesh an' blood, but the man who's fool enough
> to invest in yo' ain't bo'n yet. Ah sadly feah
> the slave-trade is OUT. Lessee . . . Hold on, Ah got
> a plan—so underhanded, it proudly declares
> its origin just by *bein'*—a MEGARIAN Plan!
> Heah 'tis. If yo' won't sell as chilluns, yo'll sell as chitlins . . .

The Little Girls recoil in terror. He puts out a reassuring hand.

> more or less. Ah'll dress yo' up in a clevuh disguise
> an' announce to all an' sundry that Ah'm purveyin' *Pigs.**
> —By an odd coincidence, Ah have the costumes with me.—

*He procures the disguises from the depths of the sack and hands
them to the Girls.*

> Heah, now, put on these piggie shoes—those neat
> li'l trottahs, an' make evvy effort to ack like the farrow
> of a well-bred sow—because, bah Hermes, God
> of Diddlin' an' Double-Dealin', ef yo-all don't sell,
> Ah'll tote yo' back to Meg'ra an' REAL Stahvation!
> —Next, slip into these snouts.
> —Now into the sack.

They obey.

> Make yo' daddy proud, guhls. Oink, an' squeal, an' grunt
> in the tones of pigs predestined fo' a highah puhpose—
> patrician pigs earmahked fo' immolation at the Myst'ries.
> Ah'll send the Herald around to summon Dikaiopolis.

*He closes the sack carefully, walks off a few paces, and attends
to the heralding himself.*

> DIKAIOPOLIS! FRESH PO'K FO' SALE! YO' WANT TO BUY?

DIKAIOPOLIS

Emerging from his house.

What's this? I don't believe it—but the signs are unmistakable:
the shifty eye, the mangy mantle on a wasted
frame, that shabby-genteel drawl—it's incredible
but obvious: a MEGARIAN!

MEGARIAN

We've come to mahket, Suh!

DIKAIOPOLIS

Well, Sir, and how are you getting along in Megara?

MEGARIAN

Porely. We tighten ouah belts to the final notch,
we reel th'ough the streets, an' then we kick the bucket
an' shuffle off ouah mo'tal coil.

DIKAIOPOLIS

Folk-dancing?
Uh—delightful! I imagine it keeps you warm in winter.
—well, now . . . what else is doing in Megara these days?

MEGARIAN

Outside of dyin', things tend to be rathuh slow.
But the Senate's fixin' to liven the State up considerably.
Just as Ah left, they were engaged in a grand filibustah,
debatin' a method of savin' Meg'ra.

DIKAIOPOLIS

Really?

MEGARIAN

Yup. The main aim is cleah: to make the FOOD
go furthah. Evvythin's set ceptin' Implementation.
They're figgerin' ways an' means to exterminate non-Senatuhs—
like me—as swiftly as possible.

DIKAIOPOLIS

. . . And thus provide
a speedy end to your troubles?

MEGARIAN

Precisely, Suh.

DIKAIOPOLIS

Somewhat desperately.

What more from Megara?

He notices the sack and jerks a thumb at it.

What's the price of grain?

MEGARIAN
We reckon it's Divine—it's higher'n Mt. Olympos.

DIKAIOPOLIS
Of course. . . . I presume you must have *salt* in that sack?

MEGARIAN
Well, Ah might—ef yo' Athenians hadn't blockaded
ouah mines fo' the past two yeahs.

DIKAIOPOLIS
You've brought *garlic,* then?

MEGARIAN
Well, Ah might—ef yo' Athenians hadn't raided
ouah fields fo' the past six yeahs. Not that Ah'm complainin',
but yo're more mice than men. Evvy attack,
yo' grub out those cloves. The whole plantation's perforated.

DIKAIOPOLIS
I give up—what DO you have in the sack?

MEGARIAN
Heah, Suh,
are Pigs fo' sackifice at the Myst'ry Rites.

DIKAIOPOLIS
Excellent!
Display them.

MEGARIAN
Ah assure yo', Suh, they're beauties. But since
yo're not the type to buy a pig in a poke—
He pulls the First Little Girl from the sack.
you jus' poke away, Suh! Feel it out, an' probe.
Yo'll find it Juicy! Tenduh! Satisfaction Guaranteed!

DIKAIOPOLIS
But I've never seen anything like this—what is it?

MEGARIAN
A piggie,
bah Zeus!

DIKAIOPOLIS
A piggie? *That?* What breed of piggie?

MEGARIAN
It was bo'n in Meg'ra, Suh—
With a sly nudge and a wink.
but, ef'n yo' want,
it kin be bred in Athens.

     —Suh, do yo' dispute mah word?
Do yo' claim this is *not* a pig?

DIKAIOPOLIS
      It doesn't look
very much like a pig to me.

MEGARIAN
     SACRILEGE, SUH!
Ah respeckfully request that yo' put yo' money wheah yo' mouth is!
A wager, Suh, fo' high stakes. Salt! A whole peck!—
An' none of yore ordinary salt, but *Seasoned* Salt!
He points very specifically at the Girl's groin.
  Now, do yo' still maintain that this luscious, savory
mo'sel is not what we, followin' the folk-usage
of the Greek people an' the genius of the Greek language,
refer to as a *Piggie?* Well, Suh?

DIKAIOPOLIS
Puzzled; inspecting the indicated spot closely.
      Not to be crotchety,
but *this* belongs to a human being.

MEGARIAN
      Ah should hope so!—
It belongs to ME, Suh! Do yo' take me fo' a hired dealuh?
How would yo' like to hear it squeal?

DIKAIOPOLIS
      This?
Squeal?—By all means, yes!

MEGARIAN
     —Quickly, dahlin
piglet, give us a squeal.
*Dumb with fright, the Girl shakes her head. He changes to a
vicious aside.*
     Yo' REFUSE? Yo' stay
shet up, yo' no-count trash? Bah Hermes, God
of Conductin' the Dead to Hades, Ah'l tote yo' back
to the Ole Plantation!
FIRST LITTLE GIRL
     Oink! Oink! Oink!
The Megarian turns expansively to Dikaiopolis.
  Now, *that,* Suh, is a *Piggie!*

DIKAIOPOLIS
     For the moment, you have me convinced.
It does appear to be a pig.

MEGARIAN

An' in five mo' yeahs,
ef it's constantly crammed, it'll swell to the puhfeck facsimile
of its mothuh, an' fulfil its Destiny, Suh.

As a cunt.

DIKAIOPOLIS

That's all very interesting, but this is *not* a sacrificial
animal.

MEGARIAN

Ah disagree, Suh. Would yo' kindly info'm me *why*
it's not sackificial?

DIKAIOPOLIS

Pigs for the Mysteries must
be perfect specimens—and this one is deformed. It possesses
no trace of a tail.

MEGARIAN

But that's not bein' DEFO'MED!—
It's teeny yet. Howevah, when it's grown to the bloom
of glorious sowhood, it *will* acquiah a tail—
monstrous, an' thick, an' red.

He produces the Second Little Girl from the sack.

Might yo' be willin'
to fatten anothuh? Ef yo' want, heah's a beautiful po'kuh.

DIKAIOPOLIS

Looking from one Little Girl to the other.

What a close resemblance—they appear to have more than country
in common. Could this be a case of congenital relationship?

MEGARIAN

Striking a tragic attitude.

In the words of that immo'tal bahd (who shall be nameless):
delivuhed of the self-same dame an' self-same siah,
Suh! An' once it swells, an' downs itself
with hair, yo'll find no prettiuh piece of po'k,
f'um chine to chin, to spread on the altuh and sackifice
to Aphrodite.

DIKAIOPOLIS

Pardon—a correction. Pigs are sacrificed
to *Demeter*—never to Aphrodite.

MEGARIAN

                         Beggin' *yo'* pahdon,
but when this pig is impaled, it'll be in the rites
of Aphrodite, an' Aphrodite alone.

Conspiratorially.

                         But why delay
yo' delights until they're grown? Ah tell yo' truly—
theah is nothin' mo' sweet or tenduh than a pigmeat bahbecue:
thet juicy pigmeat done to a turn on yo' spit.

DIKAIOPOLIS
Are these pigs weaned?

MEGARIAN

                    Ah hope to tell yo' they are, Suh!
These pigs don't need theah daddy in orduh to eat!

DIKAIOPOLIS
Weaned from their daddy?

MEGARIAN

                     Precisely—yo' know the proverb:
Theah's no separatin' a sucklin' pig f'um its pap.

DIKAIOPOLIS
And what is their favorite food?

MEGARIAN

                   They're mighty peckish.
Whatevah yo' give 'em—just hold it out, 'n' they'll gobble it.
Ask them yo'self.

DIKAIOPOLIS
To the Little Girls.

             Soo, pig! Soo, pig!

LITTLE GIRLS

                      Oink!

DIKAIOPOLIS
Tell me—do you like peapods?

LITTLE GIRLS

                  Oink! Oink!

DIKAIOPOLIS
So? How about cockles?

LITTLE GIRLS

            Oink! Oink!

DIKAIOPOLIS

                   Nuts?

LITTLE GIRLS
Oink! Oink! Oink!

DIKAIOPOLIS
Prickly pears?

LITTLE GIRLS
Oink! Oink! Oink!

DIKAIOPOLIS
Well—what do you say
to a succulent, sappy, juice-filled, well-stuffed, six-inch
FIG?

LITTLE GIRLS
Wildly jumping up and down.
OINK! OINK! OINK! OINK!

*The Megarian abandons all pretense and throws himself down beside
his daughters, startling Dikaiopolis considerably.*

DIKAIOPOLIS
—What's this? Do *you* want a fig, too?

MEGARIAN
OINK! OINK!

DIKAIOPOLIS
Surveying the three.

Fascinating reaction. To elicit the shrillest of squeals
from you, I have merely to pronounce the solitary syllable,
Figs, and. . . .

MEGARIAN AND LITTLE GIRLS
OINK! OINK! OINK! OINK!

DIKAIOPOLIS
Calling into the house.

Bring the piglets some figlets.
—I wonder, will they really eat them?

*A slave emerges from the house with a dish of figs, places it
before the Little Girls, then jumps back and races into the
house as they dive for it and begin gobbling. The Megarian
daringly reaches in and abstracts a fig, then removes himself
to safety. Dikaiopolis stares astounded at the Little Girls.*

Shades of Herakles! Listen to the scrunch of those jaws!
What untamed gluttony—what passionate, lawless guzzling!
Domestic swine?
They're wild! Wart hogs?
—No, PECCARIES!

MEGARIAN

That may be, Suh, but they didn't peck 'em *all* down—
as witness this solitary fig. Appropriated bah me.

He holds up the fig, looks at it lovingly, pops it into his mouth,
and swallows it.

DIKAIOPOLIS

I am forced to admit that I have never seen a more charming,
urbane, and polished pair of slubbering swine.
—I wish to purchase your pigs, Sir. Name your price.

MEGARIAN

Taking a tablet and stylus from his cloak, he begins to figure.
After a long pause, he looks up slyly.

Friend, Ah'll be candid. Ah can't affo'd to haggle.
Ah'm ovah a barrel.—Now, take that fust pig.
Absolutely the lowest Ah kin possibly go on her is

With the air of a man forced against his will to deal in billions.

A Bunch of Gahlic!—Ah'm adamant, Suh! Ah can't
be moved!

Perceiving that Dikaiopolis is not protesting, he points to the
Second Little Girl.

Ah'll throw *her* in fo' one Peck of Salt.
Suh, theah's mah rock-bottom offuh—Take it or Leave it!

DIKAIOPOLIS

Sir, you have found yourself a buyer. Wait here.

He enters the house.

MEGARIAN

Done, Suh!

In a transport of joy, he begins to stuff the Little Girls back into the sack.

O Hermes, God of Bahgains an' Mahk-Ups,
fo' such a princely price as this may Ah dispose
of the Fam'ly Honuh, the Ole Plantation, mah wife,
an' mah deah ole mammy—bless her glutton heart.

As he finishes replacing the Little Girls in the sack, an Informer
enters briskly from the right and accosts him. The Informer has a
loud voice, an official manner, and a small phallus.

INFORMER

You, there! Occupation? Nationality?

MEGARIAN

Ah travel in pigs, Suh.

F'um Meg'ra.

INFORMER

Ah-hah! As I thought.

I HEREBY DENOUNCE

THESE PIGS AS *MEGARIAN CONTRABAND!*

—Incidentally, you, too.

He grabs the sack and makes as if to drag it off, right.

Come along!

MEGARIAN

Heah we go again—INFO'MUHS!

Thet infamous fount an' origin of all ouah mis'ries!

—Is the Wah stahtin' up again befo' it's ovah?

He grabs the sack and pulls in the opposite direction.

INFORMER

This Curious Affinity for Megarian Causes can only
bring you to grief!

HAND OVER THE SACK—THAT'S AN ORDER!

*The tug-of-war continues, to the shrill accompaniment of the Little
Girls' cries. At length, nutrition tells, and the well-fed Informer,
gaining the upper hand over the emaciated Megarian, drags both him
and his sack toward the right.*

MEGARIAN

DIKAIOPOLIS!

DIKAIOPOLIS!

HALP! AH'M BEIN' CONFISCATED!

DIKAIOPOLIS

Rushing from the house with a bag of garlic and bag of salt.

By whom? Who's turning you in?

He sees the Informer and stops.

Where's the Board

of Trade?

*He drops the bags on the stoop, picks up the paddle, and,
swishing it, advances on the Informer.*

I request a ruling on these Informers.

Bar them from the Mart!

*Savagely arrived before the terrified Informer (who has loosed
his hold on the sack), he stops in astonishment, and indicates, with a
wave of the Board of Trade, the small phallus of his intended victim.*

—Have you no pride in your tools?

A finger-man with a digit like that? How can you shine
as Justice's Hurricane Lamp—without a wick?

He brandishes the paddle. The Informer backs away nervously.

INFORMER

STOP! You can't beat a man for exposing the enemies
of Athens! I was only performing a patriot's duty!

DIKAIOPOLIS

If expose you must, I suggest, my Patriot Beauty,
you expose yourself. But not here—unless you want
to lose your scanty equipment. HURRY—OUT!

*He beats the bawling Informer out of the market area and off the
stage, then returns to a still shaken Megarian.*

MEGARIAN

Mah sympathy to Athens, Suh. These Info'muhs—what a civic
affliction!

DIKAIOPOLIS

Retrieving the bags from the stoop.

Cheer up, Megarian. Hand over the piggies;
here's your price. Take your garlic—and your salt—
and all Good Luck go with you back to Megara!

MEGARIAN

Mournfully.

Good Luck just isn't ouah National Fashion, Suh—
it's not the Megarian Way.

DIKAIOPOLIS

Damn me for a busybody!
Please don't be offended, Sir. If Good Luck bothers you,
I'll take it back—I'll even wish it on myself!

*The Megarian smiles broadly. He opens the bags, tries the contents,
then turns to his daughters and makes a manful attempt at a sorrowful
farewell—an attempt which is hampered by his constant salt-eating.*

MEGARIAN

Yo' po' li'l piggies, abandoned to be banged around
f'um pillah to post without a fathah, Ah leave you
this lump of advice: Nevvuh . . . *yum* . . . fo'get . . . *yum* . . .
throughout yo' lives . . . *yumyumyum* . . . that a slice of bread
makes mighty fine eatin' with salt—ef they give yo' any.

*He saunters off right, eating. Dikaiopolis looks after him,
shakes his head, then conducts the Little Girls into his house.
A pause, and the Chorus forms.*

FIRST SEMICHORUS

Pointing with pride at Dikaiopolis' house.

His Marketing Acumen shows the Acme of Finesse.
His Luck, and Pluck, and Policies can only spell SUCCESS!

See how he undertakes
these radical techniques.
Informers caught within his street will have to stand for weeks!
While he can sit at ease upon his assets as they swell,
because his law of Commerce reads: RESTRICT YOUR CLIENTELE!

SECOND SEMICHORUS
To the audience, intimately.*
Imagine if you can, Dear Shopper, just what this can mean
for YOU: No thugs will pinch your lunch! What's more, you'll go home
clean:
your cloak not soiled with scores
of sticky souvenirs—
KLEONYMOS's cowardice or PREPIS' vile amours.
Nor will you have to fumigate and disinfect the traces
of courtroom-sick HYPERBOLOS and his contagious cases!

FIRST SEMICHORUS
Your tortured nose can take a rest: It won't meet in this mart
that poet who offends in both his armpits and his art,
that overfacile scratcher,
that drooling fossil lecher,
his head no balder than his name is void of any virtue,
that staggering aesthetic zero, mighty moral minus,
and ninety-year-old nullity
(we mean, of course, KRATINOS!*)

SECOND SEMICHORUS
No character-assassins will amuse the noonday rush
and ridicule your foibles with their feelthy pen or brush.
Not that disgusting person
the pornographic PAUSON,
that living, breathing synonym for Ultimate Perversion;
nor shriveled-up LYSISTRATOS, the dyed in vice, the dirty—
whose phthisic fast days every month amount to more than thirty!

ENTIRE CHORUS
We hymn and celebrate
the Secret of his Might:
THE CUSTOMER—if wrong ones are debarred—IS ALWAYS
RIGHT!

*A languid Theban, carrying a tiny bunch of mint, enters from the
right. He is followed by his personal slave, Ismenias, who struggles
under a towering load of comestibles, mostly birds. Bringing up the*

*rear of this procession is a cluster of flute players, piping away
at what might pass for a march. They continue playing even when the
Theban and Ismenias stop within Dikaiopolis' market place. Ismenias
unloads his burden.*

THEBAN*

I say, this Trade *is* fatiguing, what? I rawthah feel
as though I'd maimed my shouldah.
He hands the bunch of mint to the still struggling Ismenias.

                             Ismenias, old thing,
do try to deposit this gently. Mustn't splinter
our mint, you know.
To the flute players.

                      I say, you chappies with the whistles,
you've been awf'ly decent to tweet us all the way from Thebes,
but could we have another tune? Something spicy, don't you know?
Could you whistle up *"The Sphinx's posterior opening . . ."?*

*The flute players try. Their resultant cacophony brings Dikaiopolis
from the house. He lays about him with the paddle.*

DIKAIOPOLIS

STOP! A plague of crows on this plague of locusts!
I'm finished with screeching flutists, with Chairis and his tribe—
so OUT! Remember, insecticide is not considered a crime!
He shoos the flutists off-stage.

THEBAN

Dreadf'ly grateful, old boy, actually. Never
could stand that wheezing. All the way from Thebes.
Poor mint's completely leafless. Beastly bother.
To show my gratitude, anything here is yours.
Consideration, of course. But still, your choice: the Birds
of the Field or the Beasts of the Air! Or something like that.*

DIKAIOPOLIS

What's this? A highborn omnivore—a Boiotian crumpeteer.
—Good day, most gracious glutton. What do you have?

THEBAN

Produce of the Realm, don't you know—Boiotia's Best:
Reciting by rote.
    Marjoram, Carpets, Pepper, Mint, Peppermint,
    Lampwicks, Spring Chicks, Teal Ducks, Ruddy Ducks, Bloody Ducks,
    Jackdaws, Macaws, Hens, Wrens, Loons,
    Partridges, Petrels, Pigeons, Finches, Thrushes,
    Doves . . .

DIKAIOPOLIS
Rubbing his hands.

I feel exactly like Nobody in the proverb:
It's a fowl wind that blows Nobody good.

THEBAN

I say,

I've barely begun:
Geese, Weasels, Easels,
Foxes, Ferrets, Rabbits, Bobcats, Otters,
Gophers, Moles, Voles, and

Pointing to a basket.

Eels from Lake Kopaïs!

DIKAIOPOLIS
Mock-tragic.

O dealer in delight, retailer of toothsome tidbit,
vouchsafe me thy fairest morsel for mortals: grant
that I greet the Eel, if her in truth thou bearest.

THEBAN
Avaunt, O venerable emissary of the fifty virgin
daughters of Kopaïs!

Peering into the basket.

I say, old girl, could you see
your way clear to a brief appearance for our friend's amusement?

He reaches into the basket and brings out a huge eel, which he
hands to Dikaiopolis, who stretches it to its fullest extent
and continues in the mock-tragic vein.

DIKAIOPOLIS
At length, Dear Love? At last, O focus of my lust?
Dost thou return to rush the humor to mine eyes
and mouth, delight gourmets, and grace the table
of the Chorus when this play is done?

Toward the house.

—Vassals, attend
this lady! A stove! A bellows! Haste!
—Children,
come feast your gaze upon this enfinnèd excellence,
la Princesse d'Anguille, who lays to rest our anguish
after six lean, hungry years! Embrace her, children;
whilst I prepare burnt offering: this dish of charcoal.
—BRING that stove out!

To the eel again.

—O Love, henceforth may we
be joined as one, heart to heart, through Death;
and may his crimson beets lie light upon thee.

The slaves bring the stove. He planks the eel upon it.

THEBAN

Don't mean to be pushy, but, dash it all, one is generally
paid, isn't one? The Usual Thing?

DIKAIOPOLIS

Ah, but not
in this case. She's a gift. From Gentleman to Gentleman. An eel
to seal our dealings—and pay for your license to sell.
What else *are* you selling, by the way?

THEBAN

The lot, what!

DIKAIOPOLIS

Have you set a figure? Or are you set on barter?

THEBAN

Oh, definitely barter. Your surplus for our shortage, and all that.

DIKAIOPOLIS

Hmmm. A shipment of sardines? Perhaps some pottery?

THEBAN

Sorry, old chap. We're simply sated with sardines,
and there's a vile surfeit of vahzes. Any other overstocks?

DIKAIOPOLIS

Thinking.

Surpluses? Overstocks?—Of course! Export an INFORMER!
Ship him like crockery; standard wrapping.

THEBAN

Ripping,
by Jove! One could simply make pots of money, what?
We don't have any of *them!* Thebes would be *wild*
to see a monkey like that, just full of deviltry!

Enter, suspiciously, Nikarchos.

DIKAIOPOLIS

Speak of the devil—here's Nikarchos to denounce you.

THEBAN

Awf'ly teeny Informer, what?

DIKAIOPOLIS

Concentrated:
100% Pure, Perverse Viciousness.

NIKARCHOS
Espying the Theban's goods.
    Whose stuff is this?

THEBAN
                It's mine. I brought it from Thebes.
Word of Honor. As sure as I'm standing here.

NIKARCHOS
From where I stand, it looks like ENEMY CONTRABAND!
I denounce it!

THEBAN
            Oh, I say! Have you Athenians come
to declaring war on canaries? Simply Not Done!

NIKARCHOS
And I'll denounce YOU, too!

THEBAN
                Me? What have *I* done?

NIKARCHOS
It's not Standard Procedure to tell in these cases, but the audience
has to find out somehow: Gentlemen, from enemy soil,
this man has slipped in with an alien lampwick! The charge
is WICK-SLIPPING!

DIKAIOPOLIS
           It's sloppy logic—you'd report a man
for a lampwick?

NIKARCHOS
        That wick could set the docks on fire!

DIKAIOPOLIS
The docks? A *wick?*

NIKARCHOS
        So I believe.

DIKAIOPOLIS
        Well, how?

NIKARCHOS
Sound Reasoning. First, if the Theban should stick
his wick on the back of a cricket, and next touch it to a torch
and pitch it into a ditch—presuming the ditch ran into the locks
by the docks—and further, if the wind hadn't thinned—THEN,
if the wind should flick a spark on the deck of a barque,
the docks would go up in a flash!

DIKAIOPOLIS

                I never heard such trash—
to wreck the docks with a wick on the back of a cricket!

He grabs the Board of Trade and beats Nikarchos.

NIKARCHOS

Spectators! Be prepared to testify!

DIKAIOPOLIS

To the Theban.

                    Impound his mouth!

Nikarchos is grabbed, laid on the ground face down, and sat upon by the Theban and Dikaiopolis, who calls to his slaves.

—Slaves! Some straw and rope for wrapping! If I bale him up like a bowl, he won't get broken in transit.

Straw and rope are brought, and Dikaiopolis begins to pack Nikarchos, a process which takes some little time.

FIRST KORYPHAIOS

Now crate the freight with care, my friend,
    and pack it with finesse.
We mustn't have our customer
    import a shattered mess.

DIKAIOPOLIS

No fear; I'll see to it myself.
    This pot's no masterpiece.

Kicking Nikarchos savagely and listening to the ensuing muffled cries.

It's cracked, it chatters, it's charred—
    a bowl of botcheries.

FIRST KORYPHAIOS

But is it really usable?

DIKAIOPOLIS

All-purpose *and* reversible.
    A mortar for malfeasances,
crime-cup, judgment-jug,
    audit-lantern, evil-vial . . .
a patent thunder-mug!

SECOND KORYPHAIOS

For daily use around the house,
    how could you trust this crock?

Kicking Nikarchos and listening in turn.

What an awful clatter! It starts
    at the merest little shock.

DIKAIOPOLIS
Still wrapping.
>No fear. It's shock-resistant. Has
>a break-proof guarantee.
>You can hang it bottom-up without
>a sign of damage—

He stands Nikarchos on his head and continues wrapping.
>See?

SECOND KORYPHAIOS
To the Theban.
>He's done. What glorious packaging!

THEBAN
Gazing reflectively at Nikarchos, inverted and swathed in yards of rope and straw.
>How Jolly! Bringing in the Sheaves!

SECOND KORYPHAIOS
>Harvest it, friend. It's ready now
>for any sort of work—
>The Adaptable Informer, or
>The Universal Jerk!

DIKAIOPOLIS
Putting the finishing touches on Nikarchos, then standing up with a sign.
>I didn't think I'd make it; but the rat is packed.
>Collect your crock and cart it away, my friend!

THEBAN
>I say, Ismenias, old thing, would you bend down and lend
>me your shoulder again? Thanks awf'ly.

Ismenias obeys, the Theban and Dikaiopolis lift Nikarchos onto his back, and the Theban and Ismenias move off slowly.

DIKAIOPOLIS
>A word of advice.
>Please exercise a modicum of care in transport.
>The fact that it's damaged merchandise in any case notwithstanding,
>if this shipment *should* show a profit, your fortune's made
>in Informers. The supply here is absolutely unlimited.

He starts to enter his house. A Servant runs from Lamachos' house to the market place, shouting.

LAMACHOS' SERVANT
DIKAIOPOLIS!

DIKAIOPOLIS
>What's all this racket?

LAMACHOS' SERVANT

I bear the exactions
of Lamachos, who now desires to visit the drinking-feast.
Whereto, he demands from you this drachma's worth
of thrushes, and deigns to triple the price for one
Kopaïc eel.

DIKAIOPOLIS

Hmmm. Lamachos? Don't seem to recall
the name. What's he like?

LAMACHOS' SERVANT

His eyes flash fire! He knows
no fear! He gyres the grim-visaged Gorgon, and swirls
three huge, umbrageous plumes in triple terror
about his casque!

DIKAIOPOLIS

Oh, him?—Fat chance. I wouldn't
take his *shield* in trade. Let him swirl his plumes for sardines!
One word out of him, and I'll make a complaint to the Board!

*He grabs up the paddle. The Servant runs back to Lamachos' house.
Dikaiopolis surveys his comestibles proudly, then begins to stuff
birds under his arms.*

This merchandise is *mine.* I'll take it in to my home
wafted on the high panache of blackbird and thrush.

FIRST SEMICHORUS

As Dikaiopolis carries part of his merchandise into his house.
Citizens all, this man is an ace,
the sagest of entrepreneurs!
Behold his monopoly, sprung from his Truce,
on items not stocked in our stores:
pre-War delectables, tasty and choice—
he's cornered our dearest desires!
No toil, no spin—
but the yummies roll in!

FIRST KORYPHAIOS

TO WHOM IT MAY CONCERN:
BE IT KNOWN THAT I HEREBY DECLARE
H. O. POLEMOS, BETTER KNOWN AS *WAR,* PERSONA NON
GRATA,
AND ENJOIN HIM FROM THE FOLLOWING ACTIVITIES ON
OR ABOUT MY PREMISES:

A. ENTERING.
> B. WINING.
>> C. DINING.
D. RECLINING.
>> E. SWEET-ADOLINING.
>>> —Friends,
I've had a bellyful. I tried to be a True-Blue Host to WAR—
and found myself a host of troubles. He is simply a brutal drunkard.
You be the judge. It began with a joyous family feast,
food and frolic in abundance, not a worry in the world.
Life was Simply Perfect—and then WAR crashed the party
and smashed the table. Did I—Hospitality Itself—object?
Not me. "That's it; pull up," said I. "Always room
for one more, War." War mashed the rest of my guests to pulps,
and squashed all the food to atoms. "A drink, old man?" said I.
He was burning my vineprops. The place was a shambles. I smiled. A
> guest
is a guest.
>> But THEN War trampled my vines and spilled every drop
of my wine in the dust! Well, that did it. I got this Injunction.
If there's one thing I refuse to entertain in my house, it's BAD
MANNERS!

*Dikaiopolis emerges, collects the rest of his merchandise, and
re-enters his house.*

SECOND SEMICHORUS
Our man is aloft, he's on the wing
>> for his dinner; he's got big ideas.
His life has breadth, and expanse! There's a sign—
>> those feathers he dropped on the stairs.
And it's PEACE!* Companion of Kypris divine
>> and heaven's own Graces! O Peace!
>> How lovely and refined!—
>> (By god, I must have been blind!)

SECOND KORYPHAIOS
PERSONAL TO MISS EIRENE ADORÉE, BETTER KNOWN AS
> MISS *PEACE:*
DARLING:
>> HAVE NOT FORGOTTEN. WILL YOU FORGIVE?
>> MY FAULT.

PLEASE TAKE ME BACK. BIG WEDDING. EROS TO PRESIDE
   IN FULL VESTMENTS:
FLOWER CROWN.
                FOREVER YOURS.

He looks over the heads of the audience and speaks as though to
his beloved.

                            Peace, Darling, I *know.*
You've tried to hide it, but I know you think I'm just a dried-up,
petered-out, little old man, who can't give you the one thing
that every girl has a right to expect. Don't cry—it's all right.
Because you're wrong about me—and I'll prove it three times over
when we reach our honeymoon spot. There I'll plant your garden
    properly.
First, I'll embed a long, unbroken series of sprays
from the passion flower, and raise them for seed. Second, quite close,
I'll lay out a parallel plat of succulent suckers from the fig.
Third, in the center of the bed I'll raise an astounding stand
of lusty vine. And around this fertile plot, Sweetheart,
a circle of olive trees—unlimited oil to anoint us
for Feasts when we take a rest from our toil in the garden—say,
one day a month. Then, Pet, you'll change your opinion of me,
and proclaim to the world:
              "HIS HAIR IS SILVER,
              BUT HIS—er—THUMB IS GREEN!"

The Herald enters.

HERALD
OYEZ! OFFICIAL ANNOUNCEMENT:
                      THE ANNUAL GRAND
ANCESTRAL DRINKING PARTY* IS HERE AGAIN!
You're all familiar with the rules. At the sound of the trumpet,
swill down your gallons! A Prize to the first man done:
a skin of Old Dry Sack—
                    (of-guts Ktesiphon)!

He exits. A short pause. Then Dikaiopolis, loaded with fowl and
kitchen implements, bursts from his door. He is followed shortly
by the members of his household, similarly laden.

DIKAIOPOLIS
Rousing everyone to furious action.
Women! Slaves! Did you hear what he said?
                        —Well,
what are you waiting for? Didn't you hear the Herald?

ACTION!
These rabbit-chops—Sear them!

Now roast them!

Now cook the other side—

Now take them off!

Next, weave the wreaths.

Now skewer the larks! RUSH!

FIRST SEMICHORUS

I dote upon your Wisdom,
your Reason I adore—
but I envy you your Rations
considerably more.

DIKAIOPOLIS

Save your praise. You haven't see *anything* yet!

FIRST KORYPHAIOS

I bow to your logic—worse luck.

DIKAIOPOLIS

To a Slave.

Poke up the fire!

FIRST SEMICHORUS

Such range! Such scope in service!
Such restaurantial vim!
He's chef, he's cook, he's waiter.
And who's the diner?

HIM!

*A cretinish farmer, wearing a white cloak liberally smeared with
cow dung, enters from the left. Something seems wrong with
his vision; his progress is erratic and he keeps bumping into things.
He is crying throughout the scene.*

FARMER

Oh, unhappy day! Oh, Woe!

DIKAIOPOLIS

And who in the world
might you be, I beg to ask?

FARMER

I'm an onlucky man.
I am.

DIKAIOPOLIS

You'll oblige me, Sir, and keep it to yourself.

FARMER

Shucks, Friend, be neighborly. Don't keep that Treaty to *yourself*.
Measure me out a little? Five years'll do.

DIKAIOPOLIS

Just what is your trouble?

FARMER

                              I'm a ruint man. I am.
I lost my pair of bulls. I did.

DIKAIOPOLIS

                    What from?

FARMER

From Phyle. I live there. Boiotian rustlers rustled 'em.

DIKAIOPOLIS

Deplorable—a bucolic tragedy, in one act!

Looking dubiously at the Farmer's dung-smeared white cloak.

                                        But shouldn't
you be in mourning? At a time like this, how
can you dress in white? (Correction: Off-white.)

FARMER

                                    I kin afford it.
I ain't no peasant. I ain't. Them bulls perduced—
they kept me rollin' in shit!

DIKAIOPOLIS

Sniffing and backing away.

                              So it appears.
But what do you wish from me?

FARMER

                              It's my eyes. They're gone.
I missed them bulls so much I cried 'em out.
I did. So please, if Farmer Squint from Phyle
means anythin' to you, come on, gimme just a dab
of that there Peace-salve for my poor eyes. Please!

DIKAIOPOLIS

What do you think this is, you yokel? The clinic?

FARMER

Neighbor, I plead you. If my eyes git fixed, mebbe
I kin find my bulls!

DIKAIOPOLIS

                    Impossible. Remove your bawls
and laments to Dr. Pittalos—Painless Pittalos,
the Public Physician.

FARMER

        Cain't you hearken to the plead
of a friend in need, and dribble one teentsy drop
of that Peace inside of this here hollow reed?
Peace on me!

DIKAIOPOLIS

       Not a scruple. Not a dram. Not a minim.

The Farmer redoubles his wails.

Hence these tears. Hence, in addition, you.

He ushers the Farmer out.

FARMER

Onhappy day! Them poor, mizzuble bulls!

SECOND SEMICHORUS

       He can't be thawed or melted
    to share his Fluid Bliss—
    no Solvency was ever
    insoluble like this!

DIKAIOPOLIS

To the slaves.

SET THE SQUID ON THE FIRE! GLAZE THE SAUSAGES!

SECOND KORYPHAIOS

Did you ever hear such volume?

DIKAIOPOLIS

           ROAST THE EELS!

SECOND SEMICHORUS

To Dikaiopolis.

       You can choke us up with hunger
    and stifle us with smells,
    but keep your menu quiet:
    we'll die of decibels!

DIKAIOPOLIS

KEEP THEM ON THE FIRE UNTIL THEY'RE NICE AND
BROWN!

*Two members of a wedding party enter from the left: the Best Man
and the Maid of Honor. The Best Man is young and pompous.
He carries a dish of cutlets and a tubular alabaster flask.
The Maid of Honor, pretty and shy, follows him at a distance.
She stops and waits shortly after she has made her entrance.*

BEST MAN

Dikaiopolis! Dikaiopolis!

DIKAIOPOLIS

> And whom do we have here *now?*

BEST MAN

For you, my good man, Compliments of the Groom. This dish
of tasty cutlets from the wedding feast . . .

DIKAIOPOLIS

Taking the dish.

> Well, now,

I call that thoughtful. Splendid fellow, the Groom—
whoever he is.

BEST MAN

> . . . with a request. That you, in gratitude

for this dish of tasty cutlets, enable him to avoid
his Army service and bide at home in bed—
the better to pleasure his new-found bride—by pouring
into this flask one dram of liquid Peace.

DIKAIOPOLIS

Thrusting the dish back at him.

Enough! Never! Return these gobbets to the Groom!
Not for One Thousand Drachmas—cash in hand—
would I grace his wretched flask with Peace!

He notices the Maid of Honor.

> But hold—

who is this lovely thing?

BEST MAN

> The Maid of Honor,

commissioned by the Bride with a private request for you.

DIKAIOPOLIS

Well, dear, what was it? A private request?

The Maid of Honor whispers in his ear. He laughs.

Private, indeed. An odd request, but modest.
A stopgap measure that goes to the root of the matter.
Better for a Bride to keep part of a husband at home
than *no* husband at all. Why kick against the pricks?
Bring out the Peace! I'll do it. For her. *Just her.*
She's only a woman. And you don't make war on women.

A slave brings the bottle of Peace. He turns to the Maid of Honor.

Would you kindly assist me? Hold this flask. Be careful.

He pours a drop of Peace into the flask.

You know the directions, of course?

The Maid of Honor shakes her head.

                                 Repeat this to the Bride:
For External Use Only.
                          At the first sign of a draft,
confine the husband to bed. Apply in the evening,
locally. Rub in well with a vigorous stroke,
until swelling subsides. This Prescription is *Not* Refillable.

*The Maid of Honor and the Best Main exit left. Dikaiopolis turns
to the slave.*

Return the flagon of Peace to the house. And bring me
a ladle. The time grows short, and I have yet to fill
the containers with wine, and ready my weapons for the Festival.

*Preceded by the slave with the bottle of Peace, he returns to
his front door.*

FIRST KORYPHAIOS
Mock-tragic.
But lo! A wight with brangled brow hastes hotfoot
hither, mayhap the harbinger of fortune foul.

*The Herald enters on the run, races to Lamachos' house, and
bangs at the door.*

HERALD
Ah, toils,
          ho, battles,
                      ha, lambastings and Lamachoses!

LAMACHOS
Opening the door.
Who beats before my bronze-embossèd halls?

HERALD
Reading from a scroll.
FROM: GENERAL STAFF.
                     TO: MAJOR LAMACHOS, COMMANDING.
RE: OPERATION SNOWDRIFT.
                        LEAVE CANCELLED. DETACH
AVAILABLE CRESTS AND COMPANIES. PROCEED QUICKEST
WAY NORTH TO COLD REPEAT COLD BOIOTIAN FRONTIER.
INTELLIGENCE REPORTS BUILD-UP OF BANDITS. STOP
INCURSION SCHEDULED HEIGHT OF FESTIVITIES HERE.
THIS IS AN ORDER. REPEAT. THIS IS AN ORDER.

He races off.

LAMACHOS
General Staff! General Stuff and Stupidity!
Perish the purblind idiots who hinder me from holiday!

DIKAIOPOLIS
And pity your poor legions—led by a Major Catastrophe.

LAMACHOS
Again to endure the affliction of your gibes and gibbers?

DIKAIOPOLIS
You'd prefer to fight a Fabulous Monster? The Manticore?
The Cockatrice?

Snatching up two birds and waving them at Lamachos.
                              Perhaps the Flapwinged Flibbertigibbet?*

LAMACHOS
The times torment me! Woe, the tidings of the Herald!
A Messenger enters from the right and advances toward Dikaiopolis.

DIKAIOPOLIS
Well, times and tidings wait for no man. Here's mine.

MESSENGER
Dikaiopolis?

DIKAIOPOLIS
              What is it?

MESSENGER
Apologetically.

                        We don't mean to rush you, Sir,
but the Priest of Dionysos sends his compliments, and could you
step 'round to the drinking-feast and grace us with your company?
At your convenience, of course . . . but you're Guest of Honor,
and the whole celebration has been waiting on you for hours!
Those plushy couches, the cushions, the festal board,
the scents and essences, the garlands and bowers of flowers,
and all those perishables! Cakes, Pastries, Pies,
Sweets, Tidbits, Tarts—and all those GIRLS!
Those supple, sumptuous, raving beauties, burning
for your beck, crying for your call, ravenous and wild
to warble you a song, or whirl you in the dance, or—well,
if you don't come quickly, Sir, they might get COLD!
He exits right.

LAMACHOS
Alackaday! The smart of fortune!

DIKAIOPOLIS
                        You outsmarted yourself—
blazoning that bellicose Gorgon all over your shield.
To the house.

Time to lock up! Someone come pack my dinner!

Throughout the ensuing exchange, Lamachos and Dikaiopolis, with their servants, make their preparations for departure before their respective houses.

LAMACHOS

To his servant.

Break out my fieldpack! Issue Emergency Rations . . .

DIKAIOPOLIS

To his servant.

An emergency's broken out. Bring our largest lunchbasket.

LAMACHOS

Moldy biscuits, a stack of mildewed hardtack . . .

DIKAIOPOLIS

The fresh-baked bread, the buns, the *petits fours!*

LAMACHOS

. . . some lumps of salt, a bag of wormy beans . . .

DIKAIOPOLIS

That tasty filet of sole! Never could stand beans.

LAMACHOS

. . . the dried and dessicated heads and tails of scrod.

DIKAIOPOLIS

The sweetbreads *en brochette*—I'll roast them there.

LAMACHOS

The swirling plumes to deck my hero's helm!

DIKAIOPOLIS

Now for *my* birds. Let's pack those yummy thrushes.

LAMACHOS

Ah, the blazing glint of this ostrich plume!

DIKAIOPOLIS

The delicate, brownish tint of a roasted thrush!

LAMACHOS

—Avaunt, Sirrah! Cease your fleering at my panoply!

DIKAIOPOLIS

—Well, tit for tat. You stop leering at my pigeons.

LAMACHOS

To his servant.

Hither with the case that cradles my triple panache!

DIKAIOPOLIS

To his servant.

The pan and ladle for that savory rabbit casserole.

LAMACHOS

A murrain on the moths who sneaked in to feast on my crests!

DIKAIOPOLIS

If I hurry, just time for a tasty snack before dinner.

He picks up a partridge leg and begins to eat.

LAMACHOS

You gabbling glutton, forbear to mock me with your menus!

DIKAIOPOLIS

I wasn't talking to *you*. The boy here and I
have a wager going. You can hold the stakes and decide
the issue, if you wish.

Waving the partridge leg at Lamachos.
                                    Here's the Bone of Contention:
which is more delicious—Partridge or Duck?

LAMACHOS

OUTRAGE!

DIKAIOPOLIS

                    I agree: Partridge. —Pay me, boy.

LAMACHOS

STINKING PEASANT!

DIKAIOPOLIS

                        So? No accounting for tastes.

LAMACHOS

To his servant.
Lift down my deadly, lethal lance from the rack!

DIKAIOPOLIS

To his servant.
We'd better take that lovely sausage off the stove.

LAMACHOS

Grasp tight the haft, whilst I uncase the spear!

DIKAIOPOLIS

Hold on to the spit, while I strip off the sausage.

LAMACHOS

Assemble the sturdy tripods to support my shield!

DIKAIOPOLIS

Rubbing his stomach.
That tempting stew of tripe—*mine* needs supporting, too.

LAMACHOS

Now fetch the Peerless Prime of my *Apparatus Belli* . . .

DIKAIOPOLIS
Still rubbing his stomach.
> You heard the man, boy. Hurry. I'll take the same.

LAMACHOS
> The Ghastly Gorgon-Bedizened Orb of my Shield!

DIKAIOPOLIS
> That sugary shortcake for dessert. Don't forget the cheese.

LAMACHOS
> —I term that a Rank Offense—Flat Insolence!

DIKAIOPOLIS
> —As you choose. *I* call it Fresh Three-Layer Spice Cake.

LAMACHOS
To his servant.
> Furnish my buckler. In its shimmering, mantic surface
> I behold a gaffer, soon to shiver in the dock
> on the cowardly charge of Shirking his Country's Service!

DIKAIOPOLIS
To his servant.
> Ice the spice cake. In its candid, candied surface
> I behold the very same gaffer guffawing at cheese-head
> Lamachos, son of Gorgonzola.
To Lamachos.
> —Tune up your threnodies!

LAMACHOS
> Bring now my brazen breastplate against the battles!

DIKAIOPOLIS
> And now for the drinking-festival—bring the bottles.

LAMACHOS
Putting on the breastplate.
> Thus firmly carapaced shall I defy the foeman!

DIKAIOPOLIS
> A wee bit of fortification against my competitors.
He drinks from the bottle.

LAMACHOS
> Bind up my blankets tight against the shield!

DIKAIOPOLIS
> We'll have to tie the rest of the banquet to the basket.

LAMACHOS
> I hoist the burdensome fieldpack and bear it forth!

DIKAIOPOLIS

It's hard to get help these days. I'll carry my cloak.

LAMACHOS

Struggling under the pack.

> Raise high the laden shield, boy! FORWARD, MARCH!
> —"Snowdrift," quotha! Welladay—the Winter of my Discontent!

He moves off slowly to the left, followed by his servant.

DIKAIOPOLIS

> Raise high the viands—Supper is Icumen In!

He moves off briskly to the right, followed by his servant.

FIRST KORYPHAIOS

To the departing pair.

> Now each to his own, campaigners!
> May each good fortune pursue!

To Lamachos, with a gesture at Dikaiopolis.

> His creature comforts compel us
> to wonder what motivates *you:*
> Why freeze in the snow as a sentry
> and stiffen erect at attention?
> *He'll* stiffen in bed, while a beauty
> attends to his seething erection.

*No reply. The processions exit. He turns and addresses the
audience, recitatif.*

> A compact prayer *in re* that greediest of civil servants,
> that blubber-lipped bard of blather, ANTIMACHOS, son of Spittoon:
> BLAST HIM, ZEUS!
> He conducted our Chorus in last year's performance,
> and barred us from the post-play supper. We didn't get a bite—not one!

FIRST SEMICHORUS

Singing.

> We've planned a little dinner for Antimachos.
> We'll sit him down and watch him salivate,
> impatient for our subtle dish,
> a finely roasted cuttlefish
> *au gras, au jus*—and oh, so very late!

> We've planned a little dinner for Antimachos;
> at last we'll bring it, sizzling, sweet, and brown.
> The sight of squid will ravage him;
> he'll reach—but, by our stratagem,
> a dog will get there first and gulp it down—
> *Yes, a dog will get there first and gulp it down!*

SECOND KORYPHAIOS

So much for his gluttony, Gentlemen; now to do his lechery justice.
Some night, when this boudoir cavalier dismounts from the mattress
    for home,
on the way we envision him, shaken with ague, meeting ORESTES
the madman,* drunk, who will smash in his skull with a satisfying *boom*.

SECOND SEMICHORUS

    We've planned some entertainment for Antimachos.
        He'll venture to avenge his broken head;
           the moment that he topples prone,
           he'll fumble for a cobblestone—
        but grab a newly minted turd instead.

    We've planned some entertainment for Antimachos.
        He'll struggle up and give Orestes chase.
           He'll draw his deadly pellet back
           and launch his aerial attack—
        and miss, and hit KRATINOS in the face—
      Yes, he'll miss, and hit Kratinos *in the face!*

*Lamachos' Servant runs in wildly from the left and bangs at
the door of his master's house.*

    LAMACHOS' SERVANT
In the style of a Euripidean messenger-speech, with footnotes.*

    Ho! ye vassals, and ye serfs Ahoy! who habit
    the halls of Lamachos! Water, water! Enchafe
    the healing flood! Warm up about a cupful.
    Prepare ye plaster and poultice, ply splint and sponge,
    fix fomentation and embrocation! And some tape for his ankle.
    Succor our shattered Hero, our shivered Lord,
    most fell and foully pierced by a stick. He tried
    to hop a trench. Aye, and worse! Oh, curse
    the abrupt peripety, the wrenching reversal! He sprained
    his ankle. His crown is cleft. Remorselessly cleaved.
    Cloven by a craven rock. He tripped and fell on it,
    so hard that he waked the ghastly, grim-visaged Gorgon
    from her shield and snapped that great big Boastard feather
    off short on the stones. He raised his awful song:
    "Divine Effulgence, Glorious Orb of Radiance,
    O Lambent Eye of Day, receive thou now,
    at this my finest hour, my final gaze.

I leave this light. I am no more. . . ." And SPLASH!
headlong into a ditch kerflop,
                    face down. And yea,
he rose once more, to harry and rout the rabble
brigands into flight. Oh, what a charge was this!
Straight into a lance.

               But lo, he comes! Behold
the peerless paladin! Ope wide the portals, ho!

Lamachos, badly battered, is brought in from the left on the arm of two slaves.

LAMACHOS
               Cry Woe! the Injustice of War!
Racked with torture, with torment rent, I writhe
at agony's onslaught, a riddled wreck of body!
Oh, I am slain, sped stiff to ruin by the edge
of enemy staff!
               But pen me from the peak of pain.
Let me, undone, be not descried by Dikaiopolis,
whereat my woe might make me meat for mockery!

Dikaiopolis, very drunk, reels in from the right, with a whore on each arm. He carries an empty wineskin.

DIKAIOPOLIS
               Sing ho! for the breasts of a whore!
So packed with pleasure! So firm and tense! I seethe
as passion's upsurge readies me for work so bawdy!
Oh, am I primed, made stiff for love by the nudge
of a friendly bosom!
               So kiss me, Golden Girls!
Cover with love, both inside and out, the mouth
that drank the wine to win the drinking-feast!

LAMACHOS
With a horrified glance at Dikaiopolis.
               I shudder at Suffering's icy summit; my tale is told.
Cry woe, woe, for wounds which pain and pain again!

DIKAIOPOLIS
The Knight-Aberrant Lamachos! Good day, O Hero, j.g.!

LAMACHOS
MISERY!

DIKAIOPOLIS
To the First Whore, with a shiver of pleasure.
               Why did you kiss me?

LAMACHOS

ADVERSITY!

DIKAIOPOLIS

To the Second Whore, with another shiver of pleasure.

Why did you bite me?

LAMACHOS

Alas the charge! The cost! My cup runneth over with gall.

DIKAIOPOLIS

I don't know what you've been drinking, but Festival wine is free.

LAMACHOS

Apollo Paian! Healer! Send thy servant succor!

DIKAIOPOLIS

You'll have to wait for the Feast of Panacea—the All-Day Succor.*

LAMACHOS

To the Slaves.

A hand to soften my affliction!

DIKAIOPOLIS

To the Whores.

A hand to harden my erection!

LAMACHOS

I swoon, smitten by a rock!

DIKAIOPOLIS

I'm swollen as mighty as a boulder.

LAMACHOS

Wretched shall I lie in the dark!

DIKAIOPOLIS

I'm rigid. I'll lay in the dark.

LAMACHOS

To his comrades.

Tenderly bear me with hands that heal to Pittalos' clinic.

DIKAIOPOLIS

Take *me* to the judges. Who's in charge here? Award me the prize!

LAMACHOS

As he is carried off.

A baleful bolt impaled my bones and drained my soul!

DIKAIOPOLIS

Brandishing the empty wineskin at the Chorus.

The evidence of victory—it's empty! *All Hail, the conquering Hero!*

FIRST KORYPHAIOS

We bow to an elder's wisdom. *All Hail, the conquering Hero!*

DIKAIOPOLIS

What's more, I poured it neat and swallowed it down at a gulp!

FIRST KORYPHAIOS

The hallmark of true nobility! Proceed in triumph with your prize!

*A huge, full wineskin, the prize for the drinking contest, is
brought to Dikaiopolis. He clutches it, and, still supported
by the whores, starts off-stage.*

DIKAIOPOLIS

Follow my lead, and sing *All Hail, the Conquering Hero!*

CHORUS

> We gladly follow in your train
> to glorify your bold design
> and raise our panegyric strain
> in praise of wisdom mixed with wine:
> ALL HAIL, THE CONQUERING HERO!

All exit, singing and dancing.

Notes

page 9. *five talents:* This takes at face value an old solution of a notorious crux and assigns Kleon's punishment, not to some actual event, but to Aristophanes' lost play, *The Babylonians,* produced in 426. Other solutions founder on the amount, really staggering for an individual to pay.

10. *The Executive Board:* Literally, the "prytanies," the members of a revolving executive committee of the Council (*Boule*) of 500. There were fifty prytanies, the representatives of one of the ten tribes which made up the 500 members of the Council, and who convened and presided over the Assembly (*Ekklesia*) in turn.

10. *Olympos:* In the Greek, this peripatetic divine's name is "Amphitheos" —"having a god on both sides of the family." There is also a look, reflected in this character's actions, at the verb *amphitheein*—"to run around." The English "Divine" or "Father Divine" or "Brother Divine" is scarcely suitable.

11. *He begat me:* This genealogy is probably a parody and spoof of the elaborate genealogies with which so many Euripidean prologues began. With typical incongruity, Aristophanes juxtaposes the names of bona fide gods (Demeter, Triptolemos, etc.) with everyday Athenian names (Phainarete, etc.).

13. *PERSIA:* Both Athens and Sparta were in constant suit throughout the early years of the War for aid from this traditional enemy. Persia played her cards very closely, then threw in her lot with the Peloponnesians in 412, after the Athenian disaster at Syracuse.

14. *Crapathians:* This is preserved as a monument, if one were needed, to the impossibility of reproducing one of Aristophanes' favorite comic devices, the pun on proper names. The "Golden Hills," whatever they were, must have been in Asia. This attempt does not mean to imply that the Persian Empire, huge though it was, ever permeated to Transylvania.

16. *The All-Athenian Boy:* Literally, "the son of Sibyrtios," who was a noted trainer of athletes. The usual sarcastic jibe at Kleisthenes' effeminacy.

17. *SITALKES:* King of the Odrysians in Thrace, with whom Athens maintained an alliance in the early years of the War. An uneasy alliance,

evidently, since Sitalkes seemed much more interested in attacking Makedonia than aiding in the struggle in Greece proper. Aristophanes' feeling that this alliance, like the representations to the Persians, was an elaborate boondoggle, is pointed up by his making Kleon's notoriously corrupt toady Theoros the Athenian envoy.

page 23. *PHAΫLLOS:* Of Croton, probably, thrice victor in the Pythian games and possibly at the Olympian. Commander of a ship at Salamis. Aristophanes' stock example for swiftness, but swiftness of long ago.

24. *Country Dionysia:* This rustic feast, held in December-January, was seriously curtailed during the war by the necessary retreat of most of the rural population within the City walls during the winter. The other Dionysian celebrations—the Lenaia (end of January) and the Great, or City Dionysia (end of March)—continued.

29. *Breadboard:* The nearest English equivalent to *epixênon*—a chopping block *for domestic use.* This is the first of a string of devices, such as Euripides' rags, which provide the background for and at the same time undercut the tragic *mise en scène,* and thus make workable the parodies of the *Telephos* which now come thick and fast. So the same with the basket of coals parodies Telephos' threat to the infant Orestes in Euripides' play; the address on the Peloponnesian War, Telephos' defense of his (and the Trojans') actions at the beginnings of the Trojan War; the meeting with Lamachos, Telephos' confrontation by Achilles.

31. *Charcoal-lovers:* Acharnai was the largest of the rural demes of Attica, located approximately seven miles north of Athens near the foot of Mt. Parnes and consisting mostly of small farmers and charcoal burners. In 431, at the beginning of the Peloponnesian War, the deme of Acharnai had been ravaged by the Spartans and their allies under the command of Archidemos, and after the establishment of a Spartan post near Parnes, the Acharnians were forced to take refuge in the city of Athens. Ruined by the war and violently anti-Spartan, they became the most bellicose element in Athens, constantly clamoring to take the field against the Spartans. Indeed, Archidemos' strategy appears to have been based on the hope that the Acharnians might force the Athenians to offer a pitched battle with the Spartans—which would almost certainly have resulted in Athenian defeat. Thanks to Perikles' leadership, however, a policy of defensive attrition was adopted and a disastrous land-battle avoided. For the purposes of his play, Aristophanes deliberately emphasizes the extreme belligerence of the Acharnians in order to give point and resonance to the arguments of Dikaiopolis. Typically, it is only through Dikaiopolis' threat to massacre a scuttle of charcoal —the livelihood of most Acharnians—that the Acharnians are persuaded to hear him at all.

33. *Kleon:* Here, as often in the first half of the play, Dikaiopolis seems to speak in the person of Aristophanes. The legal proceedings referred to

here and elsewhere would seem to be an action for something like *lèse-majesté* brought against Aristophanes in 426 following his attack on Kleon in *The Babylonians*. This has led to the conjecture that Aristophanes played the leading role. I think this unnecessary and unlikely; Aristophanes is fond of injecting himself into other characters in other plays of his (such as Bdelykleon in *The Wasps*), and withdrawing at will, so the reader is left with that sort of half-allegory which is this poet's stock in trade. But, supposing Aristophanes *did* play Dikaiopolis, we are left with one great problem. For this to work, the audience would have to know it, in which case the anapests in the parabasis, the usual place for an author's address, would be intolerably deflated.

page 35. *KEPHISOPHON:* The naming of this servant as the musician who was an intimate of Euripides is rejected as a whim of the scholiast by most modern editors except Rogers. The servant is thus labeled "SERVANT." When the source of the objection is sought, it seems to be the undoubted fact that Kephisophon was not, in actuality, a slave of Euripides'. But this sort of sight-humor is surely part of the fun. Further, it does not appear to be what a scholiast would introduce, but reproduce.

42. *Alas, my Soul:* That favorite Euripidean device, the address to one's soul, is parodied here and at the end of the scene. For a famous example see the *Medea* 1056 ff.

42. *in groceries:* Introducing, to be picked up at the scene's end, Aristophanes' favorite gibe at Euripides: that his mother had been a vegetable-seller. The truth of this is not known.

45. *Lenaia:* This feast was not closed to non-Athenians by statute, but by weather, which kept ships from the sea in the winter, and thus kept friendly aliens from Athens, inaccessible during the War by land.

47. *from the skies:* A version of the famous Megarian Decree of 432, so strangely glossed over by the historian Thucydides in his account of the causes of the War. This translation adopts Schneidewin's *ouranōi* for *ēpeirōi* at line 534.

49. *on stage:* This subsequent scene has been inflated somewhat in the translation; Aristophanes could take Lamachos' jingoism as thoroughly familiar to his audience. Insufficient realization of this fact has led some critics to censure the scene, or even posit it as an imperfect second edition—the first edition, of course, would have contained considerable spouting by Lamachos.

51. *Purple Patches:* Emending *lophōn* in 575 to *logōn*.

53. *GENERAL:* As can be seen from subsequent developments, Lamachos is here inflating his rank, a joke which the audience must have appreciated. I have tried to point this up by the references to his probable rank at this time (*lochagos*—imperfectly rendered, "Major"). But the most difficult thing about Lamachos is his name. The root *mach-* means

fight, or battle, and Aristophanes plays on this relentlessly. If Lamachos had not been a real person, one might render his name as "Slaughter." In any case, he *was* elected a general the summer after the production of this play.

page 54. *Chaonia:* A barbarian settlement in Thrace; like Sicily here, a good destination for a boondoggle. There is a play on *chaskein* "to gape wide" as in Shambyses' characterization of the Athenians as *"chamnoprokt"* "gap-assed."

56. *ANAPESTS:* The main portion of the Parabasis—this choral address to the audience, embodying the author's remarks—was cast in anapestic tetrameter.

57. *Summer Residents:* This is a calculated lie of the translator to cover up a hopeless situation. We do not know Aristophanes' relation to Aigina. Most statements such as that it was his birthplace, or that he was a colonist, or that his father had lived there, are rationalizations, either ancient or modern, of this passage. About all we can be sure of (and some doubt *it*) is that the poet in question is Aristophanes, and not his producer Kallistrates. But he was certainly *not* a Summer Resident.

58. *and I quote:* Doubly: the passage as a whole from the mouth of Aristophanes, the italicized portion lifted from Euripides.

59. *Clock of Water:* The *klepsydra* which timed the speeches in the Athenian law courts.

60. *THOUKYDIDES:* Not the historian, but the celebrated general, son of Melesias. The process here referred to must have occurred sometime after his return from ostracism in 434.

61. *ALKIBIADES:* Athens' most famous black sheep, in his mid-twenties, was already being satirized by Aristophanes for dissolute brilliance.

61. *huge paddle:* In the Greek, Dikaiopolis swings three straps, which constitute his *agoranomoi* or "market-inspectors."

61. *Megarian:* The Megarian's speech in the Greek is quite thick Doric, made thicker by some editors who prefer to regard Aristophanes as a dialectologist rather than a comedian. I have made him a combination of Jeeter Lester and Senator Claghorn to try to realize, at least for those who share my feelings in this matter, what a Megarian accent conveyed to Athenians at this time: impoverishment and windy slyness.

63. *Pigs:* The subsequent scene depends for most of its effect on a basic pun: The word *choiros* means "pig" and is slang for the female genitalia. As there is no way to reproduce the pun in English *and* keep the sense of the scene, I have left it as a *sous-entendu* for the reader and tried to heighten the surroundings.

74. *To the audience, intimately:* This stage direction, plus "Dear Shopper," is counter to the usual interpretation, which is that the Chorus is talking about Dikaiopolis in the first stanza and *to* him in the second, third, and fourth. It seems to me that this stems from a misunderstanding of *hypopsōnōn* (here rendered inaccurately, but in the right direction, by

"pinch your lunch"), together with a failure to realize that the Chorus is acting as an intimate shill.

page 74. *Kratinos:* The aged comic poet, one of Aristophanes' chief rivals. Certain commentators, notably Rogers, tie themselves into knots to prove that this is another, younger Kratinos—who is probably the invention of a bothered scholiast.

76. *THEBAN:* Again, the Greek is in dialect. I have made the Theban into a Wodehousian sillyass to approach, according to my prejudices, the feelings Athenians had about Boiotians: effete, impossibly stupid aristocrats.

76. *whistle up "The Sphinx's posterior opening?":* The Greek has *prōkton kynos* "dog's rear." Following Starkie, I think this is a song—a dirty song, probably—and have substituted a modern, or relatively modern, equivalent.

76. *Or something like that:* The Greek has "birds or 4-winged things"— generally taken as a reference to locusts. I think that the Theban, being stupid, simply wants to say "quadrupeds" and gets mixed up. Hence the confusion.

84. *PEACE:* There is a convention, probably derived from the *Lysistrata,* that a picture, or a statue, or a naked woman representing Peace appears here. The Greek does not seem to require it. But this is no firm argument against it, except that it should probably be preceded by a parallel visual presentation of War. People seem less concerned about this.

85. *DRINKING PARTY:* The *Choēs*—"Pitcher-Feast" or, better, "Gallon-Feast"—the second day of the *Anthēstēria* or Festival of Flowers, which took place in February-March.

92. *Flapwinged Flibbertigibbet:* Literally, the "four-winged Geryon." Again, commentators see locusts.

97. *Orestes the madman:* Not an existent Athenian, but the tragic hero, pursued by the Furies, whose name had become the stock reference for "footpad."

97. *with footnotes:* The odd syntax and patchwork construction of this speech have led to the ejection of much of it by many critics—so many that I feel justified in resorting to typographical overstatement of what I believe to be the true interpretation: The Servant alternates between two tones of voice. The approved tragic declamation is steadily undermined by flat, ironic statements of the scarcely tragic facts.

99. *All-Day Succor:* In the Greek, Dikaiopolis protests that today is not the feast of the healer Paian. As the translation tries to demonstrate, there was none.

Glossary

ACHARNAI: Largest of the rural demes of Attika, located about seven miles north of the city of Athens. Its inhabitants were noted, primarily, for charcoal-burning, military valor, and their bitter hatred of Sparta.

AGORA: The main market place of Athens, used for holding trials, public debates, and the transaction of business.

AIGINA: An island in the Saronic Gulf, approximately twenty miles from Athens' port of Peiraieus (q.v.).

AISCHYLOS, AESCHYLUS: The great Athenian tragedian (525-456 B.C.).

ALKIBIADES: An Athenian politician (ca. 450-404) of great ability and brilliance. Of aristocratic Alkmaeonid descent, he was related to Perikles and was, for some time, a devoted disciple of Sokrates. Distinguished by wealth, birth, and spectacular personal beauty, he spent his youth in lavish display and debauchery (Pheidippides in *Clouds* has been thought to be a caricature of Alkibiades). After the death of Kleon in 422, Alkibiades became chief of the belligerent anti-Spartan party in Athens in opposition to the more conservative Nikias and was one of the primary advocates of the disastrous Sicilian expedition in 415.

ANTIMACHOS: A homosexual on a prodigious scale.

APHRODITE: Goddess of beauty and sexual love.

APOLLO: God of prophecy, music, healing, and light; and his two chief shrines were at Delphoi (q.v.) and the island of Delos (q.v.).

ASPASIA: Mistress of Perikles and the most famous courtesan of the age.

BACCHOS: *See* DIONYSOS.

BELLEROPHON: The famous legendary hero of the winged horse, Pegasos, and protagonist of a lost Euripidean tragedy. Toward the end of his career, Bellerophon met with misfortune, and wandered alone, a crippled beggar, shunning mankind.

BOIOTIA: A plentifully supplied state, directly northeast of Attika. Its capital was Thebes (q.v.) and during the Peloponnesian War, it was allied with Sparta.

CHAIRIS: An inept flutist.

DELOS: A small Aegean island sacred to Apollo.

DELPHOI, DELPHI: A town in Phokis, celebrated for its great temple and oracle of Apollo.

DEMETER: The Earth-Mother; goddess of grain, agriculture, and the harvest, worshipped in her shrine at Eleusis in Attika.

DEXITHEOS: A lyre player of considerable talent and onetime victor at the Pythian games.

DIONYSOS: God of vineyards, wine, and dramatic poetry; also called Bacchos, Evios, Bromios, etc.

EKBATANA: A city in Media, once the capital of the Median kingdom, and later the summer residence of the Persian kings. For the average Greek, Ekbatana was a kind of El Dorado, a distant city of fabulous wealth.

EUATHLOS: An orator and informer of no principles; it was he who brought charges against Perikles' rival, Thoukydides (q.v.), after his return from ostracism.

EURIPIDES: Athenian tragedian (480-406 B.C.) whose character and plays were constantly ridiculed by Aristophanes. Euripides' mother may have been (though this is uncertain) a marketwoman who sold chervil, and Aristophanes never tires of twitting the tragedian about his mother's vegetables.

GORGON: Mythological female monster of terrible aspect, frequently used as an emblem of terror on armor, shields, etc.

HERAKLES: Hero and demigod, son of Zeus and Alkmene: renowned for his great labors, his prodigious strength, and his gluttonous appetite.

HERMES: God of messengers and thieves; in Athens in every doorway stood a statue of Hermes (i.e., a *herm,* usually a pillar surmounted by a bust of the god), protector of the door and guardian against thieves—presumably because it takes a thief to keep another thief away.

HYPERBOLOS: An Athenian demagogue, successor to Kleon on the latter's death in 422. Of servile origins, he seems to have been a peddler of lamps and then to have studied with the sophists in order to advance himself politically. (At least these are the charges made against him by Aristophanes.) He was later ostracized and finally murdered by the oligarchical leaders in Samos.

INO: Euripidean heroine-in-tatters and wife of Athamas. She threw herself at her mad husband's feet, begging for mercy, but he refused to listen and threw her into the sea where she was transformed into the sea goddess Leukothea.

KELEOS: Dynastic name of the kings of Eleusis in Attika. The first Keleos was the father of Triptolemos (q.v.) and Demeter's host at

Eleusis. The Keleos who in *Acharnians* is married to Phainarete (q.v.) would appear, in Olympos' genealogy, to be the grandson of the first Keleos.

KEPHISODEMOS: Father of Euathlos (q.v.).

KEPHISOPHON: Secretary to Euripides (q.v.).

KLEISTHENES: A notorious homosexual, and one of Aristophanes' favorite targets.

KLEON: A wealthy tanner; the most notorious and powerful of all Athenian demagogues. After the death of Perikles in 429 B.C., Kleon became, until his own death in 422, the leader of the radical democracy and the anti-Spartan extremists in Athens. An impressive speaker and a thoroughly unscrupulous and venal politician, he was bitterly loathed and attacked by Aristophanes. In 424 B.C., thanks to his coup in capturing the Spartan hoplites at Sphakteria, he reached the height of his power; so unchallengeable was his position that he was able to persuade the Athenians not to accept the handsome terms offered by Sparta in an attempt to recover her imprisoned hoplites. Filled with confidence in his military ability and tempted by the hope of further glory, Kleon took command of an Athenian army in Thrace, where, in 422, he was defeated and killed by the Spartan forces under Brasidas.

In Aristophanes' *Knights,* Kleon is only slightly masked under the name of Paphlagon.

KLEONYMOS: A corpulent glutton and part-time informer; Aristophanes' commonest butt for cowardice (i.e., throwing one's shield away).

KOPAÏS: A large lake in Boiotia. Eels caught there were among the most cherished delicacies of Athenians.

KRATINOS: The aged Athenian comic poet, competitor with Aristophanes in the earlier years of the younger man's career.

KTESIPHON: A fat Athenian.

KYPRIS: Aphrodite, goddess of sexual love.

LAKRATEIDES: An old soldier, probably a veteran of Marathon.

LAMACHOS: An Athenian general belonging to the aggressive pro-war faction and satirized in *The Acharnians* as a blustering warmonger.

LENAIA: An Athenian Dionysiac festival, celebrated in January-February.

LYKINOS: A name, otherwise unknown.

LYSISTRATOS: An acid-tongued demagogue, evidently a starveling and a parasite.

MARATHON: The famous battle (490 B.C.) in which the Athenian forces under Miltiades crushingly defeated the first Persian invasion of Hellas.

MEGARA: The Greek state to the west of Attika. Subject first to the boycott imposed by Perikles' Megarian Decree (432 B.C.) and later to frequent Athenian incursions, plus the inroads of the Peloponnesian forces on their way to ravage Attika in the winters, it was reduced quite early in the war to extreme hunger and poverty.

MYSIA: Warlike kingdom in Asia Minor, allied to the Trojans during the Trojan War, and ruled by Telephos (q.v.).

NIKARCHOS: An Athenian informer.

OLYMPOS: Mountain (approx. 9700 ft. alt.) in Thessaly, covered at the summit with perpetual snow and reputed by the Greeks to be the abode of the gods.

PAIAN: Manifestation of Apollo as god of healing.

PARABASIS: That part of a Greek comedy in which the poet, through his chorus, directly addresses the audience, usually on political and topical matters.

PARNES: A mountain in the northeast of Attika, forming part of the boundary between Attika and Boiotia. Near its foot was situated the deme of Acharnai (q.v.).

PAUSON: An impoverished caricaturist.

PEIRAIEUS, PIRAEUS: The chief harbor of Athens; its initial fortification had been one of the projects of Themistokles.

PERIKLES: Greatest of Athenian statesmen of the fifth century, and from 461 B.C. until his death in 429, the almost unchallenged leader of the radical Athenian democracy. Of one of Athens' most aristocratic families (the Alkmaeonids), he was nonetheless the politician most responsible for the creation of the extreme democracy of the late fifth century. To Aristophanes' critical and conservative eyes, it was Perikles who was responsible for the corruption of Athens, and Aristophanes never tires of contrasting the Athens of the Persian War period with the Athens of Perikles— corrupt, effete, cruelly imperialistic, avaricious, at the mercy of sophists, clever orators, and imposters, cursed with a system (e.g., the law courts) which practically guaranteed further excesses and injustices. Worst of all in Aristophanes' eyes were Perikles' belligerent war policies (e.g., the famous Megarian Decree of 432) and the fact that, after 429, Athens was left to the mercies of men like Kleon and Hyperbolos who lacked Perikles' restraint and political genius. Like almost all the comic dramatists Aristophanes was a conservative (*not* an oligarch), and although he distinguishes clearly between Perikles and his corrupt successors, he nonetheless holds Perikles responsible for creating the political system in which men like Kleon could thrive.

PHAINARETE: A common feminine name, designed to sit incongruously with the divine names in Olympos' genealogy.

PHALES: The personified phallus.

PHAŸLLOS: A famous runner.

PHILOKTETES: Archer-hero of the Trojan War and subject of a lost Euripidean tragedy and Sophokles' extant *Philoktetes*. En route to Troy, he was abandoned on the island of Lemnos because of the stench of an incurable snake bite. Here he remained in utter indigence and desolation until the tenth year of the war, when Odysseus and Diomedes came to take him to Troy.

PHOINIX: Beggared hero in a Euripidean tragedy.

PHYLE: A rural Athenian deme, on the border of Boiotia.

PINDAR: The great lyric poet of Thebes (ca. 518-438 B.C.).

PITTALOS: A doctor, whose clientele seems to have been the very poor, treated at public expense.

PNYX: Meeting place of Athenian assemblies. Like a theater, it was semicircular and cut out of a hillside west of the Akropolis.

POSEIDON: Brother of Zeus and god of the sea. As god of the sea, he girdles the earth and has it in his power, as Poseidon the Earth-shaker, to cause earthquakes. In still another manifestation, he is Poseidon Hippios, patron god of horses and horsemen.

PREPIS: A homosexual; otherwise unknown.

SICILY: Large island, much colonized by the Greeks, situated to the south and west of Italy.

SITALKES: At the beginning of the Peloponnesian War, king of the Odrysai in Thrace and a nominal ally of Athens. Since his part in the alliance consisted mainly of incursions into Makedonia, there was some suspicion of his good faith at Athens.

SKYTHIANS: Barbarians who lived in the region northeast of Thrace. Skythian archers were imported to Athens for use as police, and thus provided the average Athenian with his most immediate experience of the non-Greek.

STRATON: An effeminate homosexual.

TAINAROS: A promontory in southern Lakonia on which a famous temple of Poseidon stood.

TELEPHOS: Legendary king of Mysia (q.v.) and the subject of tragedies by Aischylos, Sophokles, and Euripides. Wounded by Achilles while defending his country, Telephos was informed by an oracle that only the weapons which had given him his wound could cure him. Thereupon, disguised as a beggar, he made his way to Argos where, with the connivance of Klytaimnestra, he covertly took the young Orestes hostage. When the gathered Greeks were condemning Telephos for his hostility to their cause, the disguised hero made a speech in his own defense, but with such warmth and eloquence that the Greeks recognized him. When Achilles demanded his death, Telephos threatened to kill the infant Orestes. Finally, Achilles relented and agreed to give Telephos the weapon which had wounded him and which would cure him.

THEBES: The principal city of Boiotia; during the Peloponnesian War an ally of Sparta.

THEOGNIS: A tragic poet whose plays exhibited such extraordinary frigidity of invention that he was nicknamed "Snow."

THEOROS: Flatterer, perjurer, sycophant of Kleon.

THOUKYDIDES: Son of Melesias; not to be confused with the historian Thoukydides, son of Oloros. Leader of the conservative and anti-imperialist party in opposition to Perikles. In 443 he was ostracized; when in 433 he returned to Athens, he was involved in a ruinous lawsuit on the charges of Euathlos (q.v.).

THRACE: Name given in antiquity to the eastern half of the Balkans and site of many crucial battles during the Peloponnesian War.

THYESTES: Euripidean beggared hero.

TITHONOS: Son of Laomedon: he was granted immortality but not youth by the gods and hence wasted away into a shriveled old age. Proverbially, any decrepit old man was a Tithonos.

TRIPTOLEMOS: Hero of Eleusis, worshipped after his death as a vegetation god. With his father Keleos (q.v.), he welcomed Demeter to Eleusis and founded the Thesmophoria, the sacred festival of Demeter.

XANTHIAS: A common servile name.

ZEUS: Chief god of the Olympian pantheon: son of Kronos, brother of Poseidon and father of Athena. As the supreme ruler of the world, he is armed with thunder and lightning and creates storms and tempests.